LAMPL
CHURCH ~

Heritage and Traditions of a Cumbrian Parish

BETTY MARSHALL

FOREWORD BY MELVYN BRAGG

Dedication

This book is dedicated to parishioners past and present,
especially my late grandfather and father
Tom and Ted Blacklock and grandson Hamish.

ISBN 0-9547482-0-4

Publishers

Lamplugh & District Heritage Society
High Thwaite, Lamplugh, Workington,Cumbria CA14 4SQ

Artwork and printing
The Firpress Group, 5a Buddle Road, Clay Flatts, Workington,
Cumbria CA14 3YD

CONTENTS

ACKNOWLEDGEMENTS

This book has come to fruition through the support of many local people, members of the Lamplugh & District Heritage Society, the Gosforth & District and Arlecdon & Frizington Neighbourhood Forums. The latter three groups have provided financial support towards the publishing and printing costs.

Thanks are also due to the parishioners who have supplied information but are not mentioned individually and to the Whitehaven Record Office for access to tithe and will information. Thanks are also due to Bob and Martha Jackson (churchwarden) for their support; Maureen Fisher for details and information on the memorials and Lamplugh/Australian emigrants; Mrs Isobel and Kendall Bruce for access to their Wood family papers; Jane and Barrie Robinson for information on their grandfather, the Rev R. Haythornthwaite; Peter Davis for providing the location map and floorplan of the church and to Peter Ross and Jeff Seddon for proof-reading and comments.

Thanks to Lord Bragg of Wigton, Patron of Lamplugh and District Heritage Society, for writing the foreword.

The drawings on pages 1 and 28 are the work of the late Ronald Dickinson and the Society Logo is by permission of Mandy Cusack.

Thank you to the following for providing photographs: - pages 33, 41, 44, 54, 58, 60, 62, 63, 68, 69 and cover photos, Stan & Marina Buck; pages 38,47,45, Pamela M. Dickinson; page 54, 81 the late Benny Richardson, page 72 Sarah Graham.

I am especially grateful to Stan and Marina Buck, for their photographic contributions. They have supported and assisted over many years by taking, printing and collating photographs and slides about the parish and given their unstinting support during this project.

Thanks to Mrs Pamela M. Dickinson, as without her support during the research period, this book would have not been so detailed. She encouraged my research and allowed me access to the Dickinson family papers and some of the personal records made by her late husband.

Special thanks go to Mervyn Dodd, who has given many hours of his time editing and helping with the preparation of the script, making it ready for publishing.

The final thanks are due to my husband Bob for proof reading, encouragement and patient support throughout the writing of this book.

Betty Marshall 2004

FOREWORD

The history of a Parish can be a history of the people and the country. Betty Marshall brings these strands together quietly and effectively and with the sort of detail that fascinates everyone interested in their own patch.

The place in which we spend our lives can have enormous meaning for us. People in that necessarily circumscribed territory are not only neighbours and friends, but also the temporal and temporary representatives of those who have flowed over those few acres through the centuries. We like to feel their continuing presence, to find footprints and traces, taking us through the past on our own land.

Lamplugh, as we see in this book, is an ancient place with an intriguing story to tell. The church has been its keystone. It is remarkable that the exploration of one building can yield so much about the lives of so many over such a long period.

My own association to Lamplugh is through family and visiting. My father used to come to Lamplugh for his holidays. So did I. First with my mother during the Second World War, to Lund Cottages, the house of my Aunt Mary – my father's sister. She had married Bob Stephens. He worked locally all of his life. Their three children grew up in Lamplugh.

In the 1960s I rented a cottage in the Lund and I have vivid memories of Blake *(Fell)* and Cogra Moss, the people and the pubs – all of which I drew in on for my novel 'The Hired Man.'

My father had another sister in Kirkland (another part of the story). I also stayed there, again very happily. So it was a great pleasure to go way beyond my own impressions and meet the past from Gospatrick in 1150 to the present day.

This book gave me a great deal of pleasure. I hope other readers enjoy it as much as I did.

Melvyn Bragg

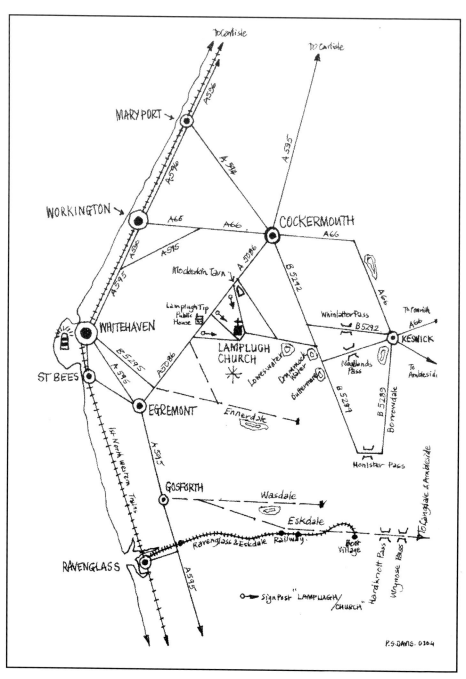

Location of Lamplugh Church, Cumbria

INTRODUCTION

Nestling 'neath the fells on the western boundary of the Lake District National Park, standing proud and high is the Parish Church of an ancient settlement called Lamplugh. This large parish originally developed from four townships, consequently having no one main focal point, only several hamlets within its boundaries. The 'church area' historically is one of these focal points.

The writing of this book grew out of a book published in 1970, now long out of print, along with a desire to write a more detailed edition. This book is not just the history of the church, but includes customs and traditions of our parish heritage. These customs and traditions are not all unique to Lamplugh; many Cumbrian settlements share the same traditions and have similar histories. Old customs are now disappearing. Life is changing and moving at a quicker pace. Many areas of Cumbria are not as isolated as even thirty years ago. Travel to all corners of the world is more common now to many rural area residents. Newer technology, whether it is the use of computers, availability of cars, better roads or air travel, has been a huge influence on present day generations.

Visitors are now discovering West Cumbria as an area worthwhile of exploring when visiting the better known Lake District. West Cumbria cannot perhaps claim the same beauty as the central fells and lakes but it does have the advantage of the Irish Sea, the Western fells and lakes all being very close.

When following the 'Red Rose' alternative tourist route from Cockermouth on the A5086 towards Egremont, the church is signposted close to the parish boundary. It stands opposite the gateway into Lamplugh Hall, which was once the seat of the ancient Lamplugh family. So this book about the Church, dedicated to St Michael and All Angels, is intended for the people of the Parish of Lamplugh, its visitors, for those who have past connections, those who are interested and for those who have come to love the area.

There is much heritage in this area of Cumbria yet to be recorded so this is a small attempt to address this. The recently formed Lamplugh & District Heritage Society (2001) seeks to create interest and add knowledge for the interested inhabitants of the district. Hopefully some members will feel inspired to record some findings to make permanent records for present and future generations.

Betty Marshall

2003

First view of Lamplugh Church when approaching from the Red Rose tourist route.

GUESTS ATTENDING CENTENARY PRESENTATION SUPPER, 1970
Left to right – Back row. George Ogilvie, Billie Sewell, Ronald Dickinson, Rev Leslie Goddard, John Stalker. Mrs Thorpe, Marjorie Jamieson, Tom Jamieson, Christopher Binns.
Front Row Pamela Dickinson, Betty Ogilvie (nee Haythomthwaite), Mrs E Goddard, Rev Arthur W Binns, Mrs Binns, Mrs Shuttleworth, Rev Claude T Shuttleworth.

PREFACE
"AN OLD CHURCH RENEWED"

THE REDEDICATION OF THE PRESENT CHURCH BUILDING

The present Church building as it now stands, was rededicated and opened by the Bishop of Carlisle on August 23rd 1870, a description of which was fully recorded in the pages of the "Whitehaven News" dated Thursday 25th August 1870.

> "Tuesday last will long be remembered in the Parish of Lamplugh as a memorable day. The occasion was the opening of the new church, or rather as the Bishop said in his address, an old church renewed. For some time the old church had been decaying and the late Mr. Lamplugh Raper, seeing that such was the case, left in his will the munificent sum of £2000 for the purpose of rebuilding it."

> "The matter was left in the hands of the Rev Mr. Brooksbank, the former rector of the parish, and Dr. Ainger, of St Bees, and some twenty months ago the work of the rebuilding was commenced; Mr. John Yeowart of St Bees being entrusted with the work."

The Bishop at the 1870 re-opening service which included the confirmation of some of the parishioners said,

> "that it was a singular blessing that when the old church was getting unsuitable that the parishioners had not had to go round the country begging for guineas here and five guineas there, as had many other parishes. On the contrary the thing had been done, as by the touch of a magician's wand; and he believed, that there were few churches in this diocese so good or so suitable."

It was also recorded that the collection amounted to £17/9/9d (i.e. £17.49p) and that the service concluded with the Benediction.

After the service a large number of guests adjourned to the Rectory where luncheon had been prepared for them in a marquee on the lawn in front of the house. After luncheon the Rev Dr. Ainger proposed a toast to "The family of Lamplugh" and said it was to "that family the Parish of Lamplugh owed its new Church." With the toast he begged to join the name of Mr Walter Lamplugh Brooksbank, whom they had pleasure of seeing present on this occasion. The Rev Mr Holme of Whitehaven proposed the health of the late Rev Walter Brooksbank. The Bishop also remarked in his after dinner speech that

> "When he saw the spirit which was manifested with respect to the new churches being built, and when he saw the spirit in regard to getting parsonage houses, so that the clergy might live in the midst of the people, this was a most desirable thing to do."

In August 1970 a celebration for the centenary of the rebuilding took place. As part of these celebrations in March 1970, a Teaching Mission was led by the Bishop of Birmingham, the Rt Rev J. L. Wilson, aided by the Rev J. Douglas, Vicar of Kilburn and the Rev M. Stonestreet, Vicar of Askrigg (later of Eskdale). The Rt Rev J.L. Wilson, Bishop of Birmingham, who led the mission, was a graduate of Queens College and Wycliff Hall, Oxford; Knight Commander of the Order of St Michael and St George; M.A., D.D., D.Sc. He had served fourteen years as a priest in England, and in 1938 he became Dean of St John's Cathedral, Hong Kong.

From 1941 - 1949 he was Bishop of Singapore, during which time he was interned by the Japanese, falsely accused of spying, tortured and flogged. After enduring terrible suffering and deprivation Bishop Wilson was released in 1944. He took two months' rest and returned to minister to his diocese and to the Japanese now interned for war atrocities. Many of these were to be completely

"changed by the power of Christ, being baptised and confirmed three years later."

Many older people will perhaps remember him when, as the Bishop of Birmingham, he led the prayers at the Royal British Legion Annual Remembrance Service in the Albert Hall every November for many years. (1)

At the end of the teaching mission week the children of the parish dressed in costume and re-enacted Christ's ride into Jerusalem. (Appropriately it was Palm Sunday). The walk, complete with donkey and the waving of palm branches that came from the Holy Land, started at Lamplugh Cross and then followed the road via the Hearse House to the church. Bishop Wilson and the Rev Goddard accompanied them. Following the walk a special service was held in St Michael's Church along with the assembled congregation.

On the anniversary day of the Centenary on Sunday 23rd August 1970, the church overflowed with parishioners, former residents and friends as the then Bishop of Pontefract led the service of rededication. Bishop Wilson, who had been due to lead the service, had sadly died. A confirmation was included in the service, as at the 1870 opening, and the choir of St Mary's Church, Westfield, Workington led the singing. Two Altar vases donated by the New Zealand descendants of the Rogers Family of Greensyke (two members of the family were present) and a coffin trolley given by John Stalker were also dedicated.

Afterwards everyone adjourned to Lamplugh Hall where with the kind permission of Mr & Mrs Horne tea was served on the lawn, the fine weather being most suitable for the occasion. A memorable as well as an enjoyable game of croquet was then played on the front lawn by the helpers after friends and visitors had departed.

On the 2nd October 1970, a Centenary Supper, which included a historical exhibition of photographs and relevant artefacts, was held in the W.I. Hall. Two past Rectors, Arthur W. Binns and Claude T. Shuttleworth and the then Rector, Leslie A. Goddard, each spoke about their experiences in Lamplugh. The rectors' immediate families were also present, as were members of the family of the late Rev Richard Haythornthwaite. Mr. Haythornthwaite's daughter Betty Ogilvie spoke about her father and his time in Lamplugh. A presentation from the parishioners and friends to John Brown Stalker of Mill Gill Head was made in recognition of his services to the church. He had been Sexton and Parish Clerk for the previous fifty years.

Betty Marshall 2003

References
1. Parish Magazine   Lamplugh with Ennerdale Church Council

INCUMBENTS OF THE PARISH OF LAMPLUGH

This list was compiled by the Rev R. Haythornthwaite. Mr R.F. Dickinson made additions and alterations. Additional updating by Betty Marshall.

1150	Gospatrick, Priest of Kelton
1200	Randulf
1260	Robert de Ulvelay
1320	Patrick
1377	John de Lamplugh - Chaplain was Richard of Whitehaven
1419	John Knoblowe - living 1452
1524	There was one Rector, one Curate and two Chaplains
1535	Robert Layburn - no Curates or Chaplains at this time
1595	Tristram Warwick
1596	Lancelot Fletcher - was also Rector of Dean; his Curate was Robert Pearson
	John Braithwaite - buried 1652 in the Chancel
	Philip (Bouch) Brath?
1654	Pickering Hewer, Curate
1655	Comfort Starr*
	John Forward* *Are doubtful Curates, probably Puritan Ministers
1656	John Myriell *
1660	George Lamplugh M.A.
1700	Jeffrey Wybergh, LLB.
1701	David King M.A.
1729 or 1730	Thomas Jefferson - aged 95 when he died; also Rector of Cockermouth
1729	George Mackereth, Curate
1762	George Mackereth, Junior. Curate
1768	Richard Dickinson, M.A. - also Rector of Castle Carrock
1769	John Falcon, Curate
1772	Clement Nicholson, Curate - also Vicar of Ennerdale
1806	John Gregson, Curate
1808	Benjamin Gregson, Curate
1817	Joseph Gilbanks - built centre part of Old Rectory
1853	A. F. Shepherd.
1854	Walter Brooksbank - he enlarged the Old Rectory
1870	James Hacon
1877	W. M. S. Ducat. - became Archdeacon of Berkshire
1880	James Macarthur. - became Bishop of Southampton
1888	Stewart S. Craig, M.A
1909	Richard Haythornthwaite, B.A.
1943	Leonard Argyle, B.D.
1947	Arthur W. Binns
1955	John L. Howard
1961	Claude Tone Shuttleworth: - Lamplugh with Ennerdale (1960 Benefice of Lamplugh with Ennerdale created)
1965	Leslie A. Goddard: - Lamplugh with Ennerdale; and was Priest in Charge of Arlecdon 1973
1974	Arthur Fountain. Priest in Charge
1980	Peter J. Simpson. Lamplugh with Ennerdale

Since 1995 The living has been renamed 'The Ecumenical Parish (Church of England and Methodist Church) of Lamplugh, Kirkland and Ennerdale.'

CHAPTER 1
LAMPLUGH PARISH AND EARLY HISTORY

Lamplugh is situated in the Copeland Borough of Cumbria. The parish is scattered and consists of the townships of Lamplugh, Murton and Kelton plus the extra parochial parish of Winder and Eskett, the latter being added in 1934. The boundaries of the parish stretch approximately six miles from north to south and three miles from west to east. Four parishes touch its boundaries. On the north is Dean, on the west is Arlecdon, on the south is Ennerdale and on the east is Loweswater. A large part of the parish is upland and contains Knock Murton, 1,461 feet, Blake Fell, 1,878 feet and Owsen Fell, 1,341feet.

Daniel Dickinson described the boundaries of 1664 in more detail. The following is taken from an 18th century copy:

> "The Ambulation and Bounder of the Lordship and Manor of Lamplugh, as it was made out by severall auntient men whose names are written in the margent hereof, before John Lamplugh Esquire, then High Sheriff of the County of Cumberland and lord of the said Manor, and jury of the homage, the 17th day of November in the 16th year of the reigns of the Sovraigne Lord and King Charles ye II, anno dmo 1664."

> "First beginning in the East at the Cross on Burnbank the bounder between Lamplugh and Loweswater goes from there southward on the hight of the fell as the water divides itselfe to a roubble of stones on the topp of a place called Blaike How, and from thence as the water divides itselfe to the Man of Blake Fell, from thence as the water divides itselfe to a place called Covringill Heade and from thence down the gill to the Rowne Cragg..."(2)

> "So it continues, a mine of forgotten place names, along the high ground and down to the Fell Dyke at Whythe Wath, through the enclosed grounds to Asby Beck, down to Rowrah, along to Winder, up by the fallen cross marking the boundary between Arlecdon and Frizington and over the high ground to Keekle beck. Up along Keekle and back over the high ground to Kidburngill, thence down the river Marron to the foot of Beck Snary and so up back to Burnbank again." (2)

In fact this boundary took in the whole of the common grazing which was shared with the tenants of the other "halfvill" of Arlecdon. (2i)

Long ago large spreading deciduous forests stretched through and across the parish, evidence of which have been discovered in the past. In 1855 whilst excavating for mining, workmen discovered a quantity of hazelnuts embedded in peat twelve feet below the surface.

An old rhyming couplet also quotes that:

> "A squirrel could hop from tree to tree, From Lamplugh Fells to Moresby."

It should be noted that in recent years many red squirrels have returned to live in the parish after a long absence.

Lamplugh was known to be an important and ancient place well before Norman times, but for what specific reason no one is really sure. It was Miss M. C. Fair's (a member of the Committee for Prehistoric Studies in the C&WAAS) theory that it was for its strategic position. Lamplugh stands high on a limestone outcrop, so in parts would be reasonably clear of trees, and therefore easier to farm. It would be much easier to defend than the many other thickly forested places in the area. Lamplugh was an independent British enclave holding out against the Picts, long before the Norsemen reached Cumberland in the 10th century via the Isle of Man.

Relics of prehistoric man, i.e. the Neolithic, Bronze and Early Iron Ages, have been found in the area. Stone Age men lived here but on the higher land. Evidence of this was a Stone Circle which stood in the field behind the present village school. Old maps mention the field by the name of Standing Stones. The last large six stones were still in place during the 19th century but have since been removed. Bronze Age stone hammers have been found in the parish at Woodend, Scalesmoor and Benthow.

The Roman road system met at Lamplugh too. The road from Moresby joined another, which ran through Lamplugh via Wood Moor and Streetgate to Papcastle, near Cockermouth. Place names like Streetgate and Gatra support these findings.

In Norman times the Lords of Workington would know that Lamplugh was the place where the Roman roads met. It is possible that they made a deliberate decision that this could be used to their advantage and so the manor should be held by a relative or by a trusted dependent of their family. Further evidence of the strategic importance of Lamplugh is that King David I of Scotland held court whilst staying at Lamplugh Hall when Cumbria was in the possession of Scotland. A charter dated approximately 1140 was from his court at Lamplugh, witnessed by, among others "Walter the Chancellor, Robert de Bruis, Gospatric, son of Orme, and Randulf of Linsey." Gospatric subsequently became the first recorded incumbent of the parish.

THE NAME "LAMPLUGH"

The real meaning of the word Lamplugh is not certain, but it is quite common for places to acquire names from the first people who decided to settle there. The names quite often give clues, which can also inform us about who the people were, and at what time in history the settlements were founded.

The word 'llan' or 'landa' is Celtic (descendants of the Britons of Roman and pre-Roman times) meaning enclosure. In 6th century Celtic times an open space or enclosure called a 'llan' was set aside for religious purposes and for burials, also indicating a very early Christian site. The 'llan' were at first preaching places with a cross and served a wide area. These enclosures usually preceded the building of a church on or near the same site and eventually the word 'llan' came to mean 'church'. The 'llan' also served as meeting places and a place for seasonal activities, and so through time the adoption of pagan sites for Christian worship was not unusual. The word 'plwyf ' is also Celtic for 'parish' or simply an area used by the tribes or people round about, hence Llan-plwyf eventually became Lamplugh. As these earliest Celtic Christian places most probably would have been in an enclosure, it is possible that even before the days of buildings it might have been a 'church place of the people round about'. The meaning of the place Lamplugh most certainly has nothing to do with being a 'wet vale', which is often quoted, although there is no denying it sometimes feels that the place does have more than its fair share of rain.

The Anglo - Saxons gave their names to Murton and Kelton. These families infiltrated from the south and had the farming expertise to settle on the heavier, fertile lands of this area. They settled in enclosures with houses and barns called a 'tun'. Moores' tun became Murton and Ketels' tun became Kelton. Most of the 'new' early Lake District place names are Old Norse; thus Lamplugh being of Celtic origin is further evidence of its great age.

THE MANOR

According to the earliest existing documentary evidence the Manor of Lamplugh belonged to William de Lancaster, Baron of Kendal, who gave it with Workington in exchange for Middleton in Lonsdale to one Gospatrick, son of Orme, Lord of Seaton.

"Charter of William de Lancaster, an exchange between him and Gospatric, son of Orme."

"Know all as well as those living as those to be that I, William de Lancaster with the Counsel, concession and consent of William my son and heir have been granted and by this, my present Charter have confirmed to Gospatrick, son of Orme and his heirs to be held by them of me, and my heirs, to be held by them of me and my heirs in fee and inheritance the whole of his land in Copeland which he holds me, as his right and heritage to wit the township of Workington with its belongings which I have given in exchange for the township of Middleton in Lonsdale; the whole of this aforesaid Gospatric and his heirs to be held of me and my heirs for his homage in free and unburdened and honourable tenure, in woodland and in cleared land, in meadows and pasture in ways and paths in waters and in mills in all liberties and free customary dues just as any knight holds in all my land freely and undisturbedly and honourably he rendering to me yearly new gilt spurs or sixpence at the fair of Carlisle and doing to me forensic service at the Castle of Egremont.

As witness these, Ketel, son of Ulf and others."

Orme, being the son of Ketel, was William de Lancaster's first cousin. Gospatrick/ Gospatric was therefore his first cousin's son. William de Lancaster was a great commander under Henry II in the wars against David I of Scotland, and helped to recover the counties of Cumberland and Westmorland from the Scots, which King Stephen had ceded to them in 1136. Gospatrick was also the Priest of Kelton. After the death of Gospatrick his son Thomas gave Lamplugh to one Robert, (who took his name from the township), 'on condition of him and his heirs paying yearly a pair of gilt spurs to the Lord of Workington.' (This was the rent that William of Lancaster had previously reserved of Thomas.) (3) It is recorded that Thomas, who died on Dec. 7th 1152, "deprived his descendants of many a fat acre." (3)

The grant must have been before 1181, as the Pipe Rolls* for that year state that Robert de Lamplo renders an account for forty shillings. Robert also held Holker in addition to Lamplugh, and it is almost certain was a dependent of the family of Gospatrick, and an ancestor of the Curwen family. If this is so, then Robert de Lamplugh's family can be traced further back to the ancient Kings of England and Scotland. This Robert died in the reign of Henry II and is the first of the family recorded in the pedigree, which was certified by John Lamplugh, Esq. at Dugdale's Visitation in 1665, in which he traced twenty-four generations.

Robert, who took the name of Lamplugh, was given the patronage of the rectories of "Ketells town alias Kelton, and Arlochden,"(3) but Robert by advowson, (the right of recommending a member of the clergy for a vacant benefice or of making the appointment)

"translated ye churche and gleab to Lamplugh from Kelton."

In other words he moved the church to the exact site where it now stands. From then on it was named the Parsonage of Lamplugh. His son Adam, who lived during the reigns of Richard I and King John, succeeded Robert. Adam had a

"confirmation of Lamplugh to him and his heirs, with diverse rights and immunities from Richard de Lucy, Lord of Egremont, as Lord Paramount." (4)

"The Lordship of Lamplugh in the 17th century comprised the manors and townships of Lamplugh and Murton, and part of the townships of Arlecdon and Whillimoor. Kelton which is part of the ecclesiastical and modern civil parish of Lamplugh was a separate manor and included, although the advowson had been granted to the first of the Lamplugh family in the twelfth century."(2)

*Ancient records, dating from 1130, of the crown revenue and expenditure of England. So called because of the pipe like form of the rolled parchments on which they were written.

In late Anglo Saxon England possession of a chapel built on an estate was considered to be an attribute of rank. During the 12th century most new churches were paid for by the Lord of the Manor, who endowed the land known as glebe land (land which was to be set aside for the maintenance of the parish priest) and a priest's house. Thereafter the lord claimed the largest portion of the church tithes and dues from the parish and exercised his rights, which allowed him the right to select a priest. This was known as the law of advowson.

St Michael's Church eventually became part of the Diocese of York, but when in 1541 Chester became a new Bishopric, the church at Lamplugh joined this diocese and remained within it until 1850. It was then transferred to the Bishopric of Carlisle where it remains. Some written records can still be found in the former bishopric archives.

References

2.	Dickinson, D.	Dickinson Family papers, Red How
2i.	Dickinson, R.F.	Dickinson Family papers, Red How
3.	Jackson W.	Cumberland & Westmorland Papers and Pedigrees
4.	Jefferson	History and Antiquities of Allerdale Ward above Derwent

CHAPTER 2
THE EARLIEST PARISH CHURCHES

Originally in a parish, the church authorities did not build churches. The local lord of the manor built them, and they were essentially owned and operated by that lord. They were quite frequently located on pre-Christian sites of spiritual significance, taking advantage of the people's existing attachment to a particular place. Worship was carried on in that same place, only there was then a Christian input. Churches then, and are still, almost always orientated so that the main altar is placed at the east end of the church, to be facing Jerusalem, not the rising sun as is frequently believed. Even if the altar end of the church is not literally the east, it is called the "East end".

The term 'parish' originally meant an administrative district. When this was applied to a church it often meant it was the territory of a bishop. Some historians argue that the parish boundaries were originally those of Anglo - Saxon manors. The authority of the lord and the church parish overlapped before the Norman takeover of Cumbria after 1100. An accepted way of becoming a thegn (a man who held land from the king by military service, ranking between ordinary freeman and hereditary nobles) was to build a church especially one with a tower. Towers were refuges in case of a Viking raid or invasion (between 850 and 950). The thegn had the power to install a priest of his own choosing, change the priest at will, and even dismantle the church if he saw fit.

In the North of England the Celtic influence led to many parish churches being built. These churches were mostly narrow, tall and rectangular with doors on the sides. However, despite the later victory of the Roman Church over the Celtic Church, it was the Celtic model that became the norm for parish churches in Northern England.

"In Cumbria there is no real tradition in church architecture mainly because the dales were mostly poor. Slate the most common building material was found not to be a good material for building in the medieval style, and there was frequently great poverty. Churches fell into disrepair, and had to be rebuilt, or were too small and had to be enlarged. Where many dale churches do have 12th or 13th Century origins, only a few remain in anything like their original state. More 'relatively recent' churches in Cumbria have towers, some of them fortified, but only a few have steeples. Many Victorian churches were built by rich landowners that wanted their own church near to the house for the use of themselves and their staff." (5)

LAMPLUGH PARISH CHURCH

The first church in the parish was in Kelton at Kirkland hence the name of Kirk (church) land and it was probably built before the Norman invasion. The site is said to have been close to that of the present Mission Room. The part field in which the Mission now stands was called Priest How. The first church in Lamplugh would probably not be built of stone but be constructed with either wood or with wattle and daub and have a thatched roof. There were very few stone churches built before the 11th century. Inside it would almost certain to be open, flagged and contain no pews as the congregation at that time only stood or knelt in the nave during the services. The paving on the church floor was laid so that it could be lifted for burials. Neither would there be a pulpit. At a later time there might have been installed a few stone benches around the inside walls for the older people to sit on. It was only during the English Reformation in the 16th century from the reign of Henry VIII onwards that churches began providing some form of seating. Trestles were the most popular as they could be moved when the nave was required for other purposes. From the time of Elizabeth I, preaching long sermons became popular. Two to four hours in length was not uncommon. This meant that the congregation needed to sit to listen, so it was during the late 16th century that long backed benches were introduced. The preacher too needed a lectern, and more often, a pulpit. So then the pulpit was added to the nave. Males and females were separated in the church, and seating was by social rank. The windows would most probably have been small slits with wooden shutters on the inside.

The Church previous to 1870

During medieval times the church would most probably have been plastered and coloured white inside and out. Few people were able to read, so it is almost certain that there would be many vivid paintings illustrating biblical scenes on some or all of the walls, e.g. pictures of the Ascension, the Last Supper and The Day of Judgement or Doomsday would be sure possibilities. It is very likely that there would be a special shrine and/or a painting about St. Michael, to whom the church is dedicated.

During the Middle Ages there were many holy days and feast days throughout the year. Some of these meant that the people were allowed days off work. From this tradition is derived the word holiday i.e. Holy Days. The mass was said in Latin and as most people could not read or understand what was being said, very little participation by the people took place. It wasn't until the 14th century that literacy began to increase, but that was amongst the wealthy lay members of the community. It was also at this time that there was a strong belief in purgatory and that the soul needed to be cleansed before entering heaven. People believed they could escape from purgatory and have their soul pardoned if they bought an indulgence, a document previous to their death that had been signed by a bishop, an abbot or a prior. Pardoners travelled around the country selling such documents. Another way of cleansing the soul was to take part in a pilgrimage to a holy place. Institutions such as chantries and religious guilds were then gradually begun by groups of lay people. For payment, prayers were said for the living souls and the 'departed'. (6)

Before the Reformation, churches were used as social gathering places as well as for religious purposes. All public notices were given out after the church service. The churchyard was often the scene for village festivities and social gatherings, as well as for dancing, games and commercial transactions. As the church was usually the only large public building in a parish, the nave was sometimes used as a ' parish hall'. The nave was unconsecrated and not under the jurisdiction of the parish priest; it 'belonged' to the parishioners. Gradually it became more and more the focal point of community life. The chancel was the only consecrated area and this 'belonged' to the priest.

On weekdays, business was transacted in the nave and agreements confirmed. In many villages it became the meeting place of the manor court. Notice of any meetings that were to take place, e.g. the manor court, was announced from the chancel. Disputants normally used the north side of the churchyard (usually unconsecrated land) to settle differences, and when witnesses were required, the tradition was to join any other people present in the nave and solve their differences there. There is no reason to think that Lamplugh Church was used differently from this. Notices of parish and church-related events today still continue to be announced from the Chancel.

THE PARSONAGE and RELATED BUILDINGS
THE MANOR BUILDINGS

The church, as in most settlements of that time, became an integral part of the Lord of the Manor's buildings. The stables and other farm buildings of Lamplugh Hall were at one time very much closer to the church than they are now. There were some buildings on the opposite side of the present road to the Hall. Within the complex, there was built a very substantial fortified Pele Tower, the foundations of which at the present time can still be seen in Lamplugh Hall stack yard. The exact date the Pele Tower was built is not known but it was probably after Robert the Bruce had raided and burned all through West Cumberland in the years that followed his victory at Bannockburn in 1314. Lamplugh was certainly vulnerable, greatly affected and troubled throughout the times of the Border Reivers until James I came to the throne in 1603, uniting England and Scotland. The raids and attacks that the Reivers made at Lamplugh certainly justified the protection of such a strong fortification. My father told me that 'the old people' in the family told him that an underground tunnel existed from Lamplugh Hall to Scalesmoor to allow a counter attack on the Reivers. No evidence of this has been found. Notes written by a member of the Dickinson Family also mention that

> "there was an under ground passage between Lamplugh Hall and the Church but it has never been found. Altho' there is a place on some stairs in the cellars at Lamplugh Hall which is built up and which may have been the commencement of it."

The present hall is not the original house as that was burned down in late Tudor times but the walls of the centre block of the present house are said to be dated to the 14th century and are five feet thick. This portion was the Great Hall where the entire household ate and most slept. It was the place where the business of the manor was also carried out. At the main entrance to Lamplugh Hall there is an arched gateway which has on it the Arms of the Lamplugh family. It is dated 1595 but the coat of arms was restored, using drawings made from the original, after storm damage in 1961. The gateway was once kept closed with large oak doors which, when open, gave access into the great courtyard.

THE PARSONAGE AND RECTORY

The Parsonage buildings were originally situated in the north east corner of the old churchyard. Some older parishioners might remember an apple tree standing in the churchyard. It is now no longer there but an old yew tree and holly tree can still be seen standing close to what was the Parsonage site. Another part of the original boundary of the churchyard wall, which enclosed the Parsonage and its buildings, is shown by the headstones which face the opposite direction to all others, these originally having been back to back with the Parsonage wall.

The following memo gives a more exact position:

> " The old Parsonage House stood approx. 25 yards north of the N E corner of the Chancel of the present Church and the same distance west from the line of the road. Its remains were demolished and the site enclosed with the 19th century extension of the churchyard. Foundations are still encountered in grave digging, and an old apple tree against the N.W wall of the churchyard (1946) is said to be a survival from the garden. An old man whom I remember 15 years ago living at Crossgates, called Jackson Hellon was born in this house (last person). The present Rectory was built in 1823." (7)

On the 18th June, 1788, the Rev R. Dickinson wrote

> "1766. Parsonage House and Outbuildings were in very ruinous condition at the death of the incumbent. There was a Barn with a stable or byer at the end. The piece of ground before the house was a piece of common or waste ground, not inclosed at all."

> "Richard Dickinson built two new Barns and " the Parsonage House from the Ground". The barns cost £40 and £30 apiece and the house £80. The workmen who built them "assures me they are well built, and they are thought to be sufficient for the living."

> " The tenant who lives in the house farms the whole Glebe of me for £6 a year, but he pays no Rent at all for the house. It is thought better that such a person should live in the house than to have it lock'd up. …. He enclosed the ground in front of the house."(8)

An extract from the Raper (descendants of the Lamplugh Family) family letters mentions in August 1857

> "that the gable end of the old Parsonage has fallen out, the chancel ceiling fallen down; a suggestion made that, a small earthquake shock in April found weak structures."

The old Parsonage was eventually 'pulled down' in 1873, following the building of The Rectory, when a new extension to the churchyard wall was built and the new burial ground levelled. The land for this new extension was given to the parish by Walter L. Brooksbank. Martin Bewick of Arlecdon built the new wall to the same height and thickness as the existing one and made good the old walls for the sum of £68. Recycled stone from the old wall and Parsonage garden walls were used. The remains of the Parsonage House and the fixtures were eventually sold for £20 to be recycled by John Branthwaite to build 'Top House' at Crossgates in 1875.

Due to further shortage of burial space in the 1970s Leslie Goddard, the incumbent at the time, informed the Church Council that an extension to the churchyard was needed. As a result another extended area was made available, courtesy of Mr E. Horne, Whinnah, but then of Lamplugh Hall, on condition that the area was walled in a similar manner to the original one. It should be noted that then there was no definite written or recorded plan of the churchyard.

> "Building of the new Rectory was begun in the Spring of the year 1823, an exchange having been effected between John Raper, of Lotherton Esq. and Joseph Gillbanks,

Rector of Lamplugh; for the former to have the ancient glebe and the Old Parsonage, and the latter to accept a field called Green Croft, with a new dwelling house and out offices in lieu thereof. The new Rectory was taken for occupation and accordingly taken possession of by Jos. Gillbanks and his family on the 20th day of March 1824". (9)

Walter Brooksbank, who was a Lamplugh family descendant and also the Rector, enlarged the new Rectory. This extension was known to be used for the servant quarters, and was later changed to become an adjoining cottage. Sadly it was decided by the church authorities in 1958 that the Rectory had to be sold publicly. This was at the time of the joining of St Michael's ecclesiastical parish with that of St Mary's, Ennerdale. Ennerdale Vicarage then became the residence of the incumbent.

The rectory changed ownership and became known as 'The Old Rectory.' The extension that had been used for the servant quarters was demolished in 1959 by its new owner David Scott–Gatty. It passed into the hands of Peter and Greet Salmon and then lastly to Keith and Gill McNeil. The Rectory has now been resold to a developer who converted it into adjoining houses and the barn and stables into dwellings. Several houses are also being built in the Rectory grounds.

An agreement had previously been made that a new rectory was to be built somewhere in the central area of the two parishes, but later decisions resulted in a new Rectory being built at Vicarage Lane in Ennerdale Bridge in the latter part of the 1990s.

References

5.	www.vjsitcumbria.com	
6.	Hobbs, Jeff.	Parishes (Internet)
7.	Dickinson R. F.	R.F Dickinson, Red How, Family papers.
8.	Dickinson, Rev R.	R.F. Dickinson, Red How, Family papers
9.	Bruce K.W. & M.I.	Mill How, Wood Family Papers

CHAPTER 3
CHURCH ATTENDANCE

Up to the latter part of the 12th century most men quite happily rode as far as twelve miles to church if necessary. In medieval times, going to church for many was infrequent and often in the form of a 'holiday excursion.' There were no hardships except for funerals, when sometimes the deceased's body had to be carried many miles to the appropriate consecrated burial ground of the mother church. Loweswater and Ennerdale for example were chapelries, where the right of burial was reserved for the Mother church, which in their case was St Bega's at St Bees.

Many medieval parishes were often remote upland areas so trackways called Corpse Roads developed along these uplands and valleys. Corpse Crosses or Corpse Rests were built along the trackways at strategic points. Here the body could be placed so that the bearers might have a breathing space and a rest. The bodies were mostly encased in a wicker or basketwork shroud, which was carried on the shoulders. Bereaved families from the farmsteads had to arrange for the bearers to carry their loved ones along these trackways, which could be hazardous, especially in the winter months. The journeys could take as long as two days.

THE LAMPLUGH CORPSE ROAD AND REST

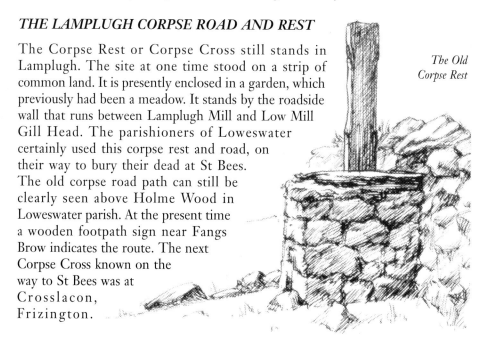

The Old Corpse Rest

The Corpse Rest or Corpse Cross still stands in Lamplugh. The site at one time stood on a strip of common land. It is presently enclosed in a garden, which previously had been a meadow. It stands by the roadside wall that runs between Lamplugh Mill and Low Mill Gill Head. The parishioners of Loweswater certainly used this corpse rest and road, on their way to bury their dead at St Bees. The old corpse road path can still be clearly seen above Holme Wood in Loweswater parish. At the present time a wooden footpath sign near Fangs Brow indicates the route. The next Corpse Cross known on the way to St Bees was at Crosslacon, Frizington.

This does not stand on its original site. It was more of an ecclesiastical design and on the Celtic cross top was a special area to place a book while the priest said prayers.

The Lamplugh Corpse Rest is quite plain but functional and has in the centre of a slab of stone, a pillar of sandstone four feet five inches high and nine and a half inches square, partly chamfered on its edges and bearing on its top marks of a sundial plate. The pillar fits the socket hole well. The difference between the workmanship and the rude slab of masonry below is marked. Why should a sundial require such an enormous base or be perched so high it would be necessary to climb up to see the time? The pillar appears to be of a later date than the base.

FUNERAL CUSTOMS

"The making of a will that paid obligations to God and to man should always be followed by a good funeral" (Stephen Friar: - Companion to the English Parish Church.)

The earliest account of a funeral in Lamplugh that has been found is that of John Lamplugh. Daniel Dickinson 1636 - 1699 in his diary "Life in a Cumberland Village in the 17th Century" gives an account of the funeral customs of that time.

" Thursday the 6th December 1688. John Lamplugh of Lamplugh Esquire, died and was buried on Sunday, the 9th of December1688 in the chancel of the church of Saint Michael in the Parish of Lamplugh. At his funeral was given to all gentlemen and women each a sprig of rosemary and bay then each a glass of sack, then burned claret wine in silver "tansketts" and then to everyone of them a large paper of sweetmeats all of which were by the hands of Daniel Dickinson and John Fawcett. To the servants and their wives that were there was given bread and beer, burned wine in silver tumblers, one penny wheat cake and one biscuit, to each, and all other persons had brewed beer wine and cakes and biscuit."(10)

" to Mr. Gaven Noble, who preached the funeral sermon, was given a scarf and hatband and gloves. To Mr. Lawson, Mr.Fletcher, Mr Senhouse. Mr Darcy Curwen, Mr Joseph Patrickson, Mr. Lamplugh, Ribton, Mr Edward Lamplugh and Mr. George Lamplugh who were bearers of the corpse, each of them had a scarf and gloves. Richard Lamplugh Jnr. received a hatband.

William Dennison, schoolmaster received a hatband and gloves, Daniel Dickinson, coat, britches, doublet, hat and band, gloves and stockings."(10)

For poorer members of society a funeral would be far from such a lavish occasion. However, the more affluent mourners were expected to give money, food and mourning clothes to the poor on the day of the funeral. The poor also received gifts of food, money and clothes on the third, seventh and thirtieth days of mourning. This practice was gradually replaced by a 'feast' for the chief mourners who were following the funeral. A diminished form of this custom still survives today.

In 'Jollie's Sketch of Cumberland Manners and Customs (1811),' we are informed that

> "When a person died the neighbours were called in at the last moment and assisted the family with the laying out of the corpse, which was placed on a bed covered with the best linen the house could afford. Between the death and the funeral, about two to three days, the neighbours watched by the corpse alternately - the old people during the day and till bedtime; and the young people afterwards till morning."

> "Bread, cheese and ale, with pipes and tobacco, are provided for those who attend the corpse. The friends and neighbours of the deceased for several miles around who were invited to the funeral were served with bread, cheese, ale, drams, pipes and tobacco. After the burial, a select party of friends and neighbours were again invited to supper."

By early Victorian times gifts to mourners were not so bountiful, as all mourners in Cumberland were apparently

> "presented with a piece of rich cake, wrapped in white paper and sealed, to be carried home after the 'lifting of the corpse.'"(11)

Guests who were

> "'bidden' at one time would contribute a small sum to defray the expenses of the bereaved." (12) "If a representative of a household did not attend it was regarded as an insult."

Consequently the invited or bidden people could have travelled from many different parts of the county to attend. The number of mourners who attended was an indication of how respected the departed had been.

Funeral processions were held as follows:

> "This consisted of the cortege, which would pass through the village, its approach being heralded by the clerk or sexton ringing a hand bell. The priest followed them. Next came the bier followed by the chief mourners in black cloaks and hoods, lesser relations and friends followed them. On its arrival at church the bier was placed at the entrance to the chancel covered with a pall or hearse. " (13)

In the 18th century, funerals of those who aspired to gentility were still very splendid occasions. Funeral attendance in this level of society was by admission only and strictly controlled. Resulting from this, engraved, decorative, embossed 'funeral tickets' were produced by specialist printers. These 'cards' were to be given to close relatives and personal friends of the deceased. On some occasions these were sent out after the funeral had taken place. The sending of such cards originated from what had happened in past times of mourning and was meant to be a reminder to pray for the soul of the departed. The 'ordinary parishioners' eventually followed suit and some examples of these cards that were commercially produced still exist in households in Lamplugh. In the late 1800s and early 1900s, more plain folding cards became fashionable and were sometimes printed in silver or a subdued colour. They often showed lilies of the valley or a wreath of flowers. Some cards notifying a death were still being sent in the late 1950s although by then they had no decoration and were edged with black and plainly printed with black lettering. They were enclosed in a special envelope that was also edged with black. In 1900 in Lamplugh the Tolson family had a drawing of St Michael's Church on their mourning card.

Before the funeral, a glass of whisky was traditionally given to the bearers and in some instances, to all the men present. This customary drink might have been a survival from the old Celtic influence but there is no known evidence that a wake as such occurred in Cumberland. A death in a family would perhaps be one of the few occasions when almost all of the relatives met together and in some cases it was perhaps a chance to have a day out! Family members greeted each other but before entering church they arranged themselves in order of the closeness in relationship to the departed. Then after the funeral, they most probably caught up with family news. The latter is still the norm today.

The custom of providing a 'feast' or food for all mourners continued. In Lamplugh as throughout Cumberland, this was by providing a home cured Cumberland Ham tea. Cold boiled ham with salads, home baked 'funeral biskies'* and cakes were the order of the day. It was known as a "knife and fork" tea. Many country families, not just farmers, kept pigs to provide themselves with a source of meat throughout the year. Boiled ham provided for the tea had in many cases been home cured.

The tea was usually held in the deceased person's household. It was made, served and organised by immediate family and friends of the departed. Approximately one hundred people had such a 'tea' at Starling Bank in 1947 on the occasion of the funeral of Tom Blacklock (my grandfather). The tradition of 'funeral biskies' continued until approximately the late 1950s. It still continues to be customary in Lamplugh and Cumbria to provide food, just as in most other parts of the United

---

*Home baked 'funeral biskies' were made especially for the occasion. They were large teacakes made mainly with home produced butter, yeast, sugar, salt and flour. Most people would agree that they have a 'special' taste, texture and smell.

Kingdom. However the custom has changed over recent years so that the refreshments are now served by hired caterers in a public building such as the Lamplugh W.I. Hall, or in a local hotel or hostelry. It is now rare for the funeral tea to be provided in the deceased's family home.

Many funeral services now are not held in church but at a crematorium and in many instances the ashes are not interred in churchyards. They are scattered either in a special place at the request of the departed or in a garden of remembrance which is usually a piece of land set aside in the crematorium grounds. Some churches and cemeteries are now beginning to set a special area aside to provide a resting place for the deceased's ashes to be interred. As yet one does not exist at Lamplugh.

In the 19th century a guide to the etiquette for the middle classes declared that

> "The blinds of the house should be drawn directly the death occurs, and they should remain drawn until after the funeral left the house, when they were at once to be pulled up."(14)

This tradition continued in Lamplugh and surrounding areas as a mark of respect until the early 1970s. In the days when people walked, rode horses or even cycled, it acted as a sign to passing parishioners that a death had occurred in the house and the news would pass on quickly to friends and neighbours. Many, especially in villages, would already know that a member of the household was ill and the news travelled quickly, without the aid of a telephone or e-mail!

Great attention was paid to the period of mourning. A well-to-do widow and mourners were expected to wear black. In Victorian times it was usually black crêpe that had to be worn for a year and a day. It was drab, uncomfortable to wear and scratchy. After two years, the half mourning began and the widow wore purple, mauve or violet shades of clothing. The invention of synthetic dyes in the 1850s produced a variety of shades that included violet, pansy, lilac and heliotrope. During the first year, she could accept no invitations and to be seen in a public place was in the worst possible taste. The period of mourning varied according to the relationship of the deceased. The third stage of mourning was different, as then it was the material as much as the colour that distinguished mourning dress. It had to be non-reflective so as to give a 'dead 'appearance. Jet, a variety of hard coal, was used as jewellery. Widowers however could remarry as soon as they pleased, but their new wives were expected to take up mourning for their predecessors. It was not until World War I, after the death of thousands of British soldiers during the Battle of the Somme, that these mourning traditions began to change.

Death in childbirth was a common occurrence in Victorian times and women dying in such circumstances were allowed 'a maiden's funeral'. There would be girl attendants at the funeral dressed in white and wearing a ring of flowers on their heads. It was from this custom of placing these white flowers on the graves that the more general practice and custom of laying and giving of wreaths developed.

There were also superstitions such as "No one could die on a bed containing pigeon feathers." If it appeared the person was 'sinking slowly' it was customary to remove them from the bed to the floor in order that they could pass away in peace. (14) Another custom was to cover all the mirrors in the room where the corpse was lying. It was considered to be unlucky to see the reflection of a corpse in a glass. (15)

As soon as a person died it was believed necessary to go to 'tell the bees'. A special messenger was sent to the hive for this purpose. Beehives were often decorated with black ribbons. I have not yet discovered a reason for this custom but it was known to take place in Cumberland until at least the late 19th century.

THE PARISH HEARSE AND THE HEARSE HOUSE

At one time, a hearse was a cage like structure which was placed over the bier when a corpse was brought to the lych gates to be buried. Today the meaning has changed and it is either a specially constructed motor or a horse drawn vehicle long enough to place a coffin inside. An undertaker usually owns his own vehicle.

The old Hearse House

At one time Lamplugh parish had its own communal horse drawn hearse. The Hearse House, where the parish hearse was kept in Lamplugh, was a small stone building, which stood close to Brook House, at the entrance to Whinnah Lonning. There is a signpost pointing out a public bridleway. The horse drawn hearse was sometimes taken along this bridleway to allow a shorter and quicker access to/from Asby, Arlecdon and the Whinnah area of the parish. The Hearse House had formerly been the Church school.

In 1869 a new 'Lamplugh Parochial School' was built beside Scallow Beck, now Dhustone, next to the Lamplugh Women's Institute. Following this event a group of parishioners met and formed a committee with the idea that the old building could be used for housing a village hearse. The committee was John Bowman, Cockan, Secretary; Jonathan Wood, Brook House, (appointed Keeper or Guardian); John Rogers, Millgillhead; John Porter, Cockley Gill and Henry Mossop of Kelton Head. This committee opened an appeal for subscribers to help purchase a village hearse. One hundred and eleven people subscribed, the amounts varying from one guinea (£1.10p) to one-shilling (5p). An entry in the 1869 account book states that

> " The hearse was used for the first time out in September 1869 for Richard Tyson, tailor, Kirkland, formerly of Butt. "

At a general meeting held by the subscribers, the rules and regulations for the management of the hearse and horse were made. In 1900, copies of these rules were printed. (see later.) Records were kept of expenses incurred, the journeys that were made and for whom, plus the date and the hire charge that was collected. Mr. Joseph Wood, who was a member of the committee, along with his family at nearby Brook House, were the last people responsible for the keeping of these records. (16)

The West Cumberland Times dated April 28th 1906 reports a description of the renovation of the old hearse

> " The old parish hearse has just undergone a much needed renovation. The undercarriage has been made full – lock, and the body of the hearse raised. The closed sides have been cut out and filled in with ornamental glass panels, with alternative shutters to be used if preferred. The ancient weather beaten plumes have been replaced with four carved corner pieces, also a centre cushion and crestings on the top, and neat carved ornaments (the allegorical figures of a lamb, a dove, etc.) on the outer body. The hearse has also been fitted with a new sliding bier and plated side rails."

Rejuvenation of the old hearse was by Mr. Ferguson, a coachbuilder from Whitehaven.

The last time the hearse was used was on August 10th 1951 for Jane Ann Jackson of Lamplugh Mill. The hearse had only been used four times in the previous four

The old horse drawn hearse

years. The parish hearse had hardly been used because motor driven hearses were becoming more popular. Undertakers were buying them to use as they were much quicker and versatile and could be used over a wider area more conveniently. Funeral directors arranged or in some cases also provided taxis and cars for mourners, so people no longer had to walk behind the hearse.

It is interesting to note that fashions are changing once more and horse drawn hearses are returning and are being used in towns and cities. At the time of writing, an undertaker in Penrith has bought a hearse similar to the one that was at Lamplugh and is advertising its use in the local papers.

In 1970 two decorative carvings, which had been taken from the hearse before it was finally disposed of in the late 1950s, were placed on a board that was hung at the back of the church. The carvings were of 'The Paschal Lamb' and 'Dove of Peace.' A local craftsman would most probably have made these. They were painted black to match the trimmings of the hearse at the 1906 renovation. They were placed at the front and back of the old hearse. An unknown person stole the dove from the board in the church, so the lamb was removed for safekeeping.

Evidence of a school, which was closely connected with the church, on this small Hearse House site, can be traced on maps dated from the 16th century and records mentioning 'a school' in the parish have been documented previous to this. Medieval records mention a school in Lamplugh. As yet there is no evidence as to where it was. Could it possibly have been the same site? The Hearse House/school building that was built in the early 1700s was rectangular in shape and had latterly been roughcast. It was quite plain and perhaps uninteresting on the outside but did not give the appearance of antiquity. It was similar to a small, low, field barn or farm building and it stood on its own. A passer-by, not knowing its history, might only glance at it because it was very close to the roadside, little realising what the inside had once been and what it contained. Before its demolition there was still a fire grate in situ and evidence of other doors and windows on the north and south side walls that had been closed up with stones and bricks after it ceased to be a school. The original flagged floor was still in place and lay flat, dry and true. Pegs and a rack were evident and still in place where the scholars had hung their coats. There was some graffiti, but it was mostly initials of the old scholars on the sandstone windowsills with dates from the 18th and 19th century.

After its use as a Hearse House, the church rented it out for other purposes. A local farmer stored machinery and hay there. In the mid 1990s the building was damaged when thieves stole the slates off the Whinnah Lonning side of the roof and left it open to the elements. The will to retain the Hearse House diminished and offers to do repairs were not supported by the Church Council, so the roof was not replaced. Sadly it became an underrated heritage landmark of the parish and was demolished in the late 1990s. Only a triangular grassy patch with a small wall remains. A commemoration stone to mark the significance of the area has been placed there by the Bruce family, descendants of the Wood Family, to mark the site. (May 2001). The stone used was one taken from the original building and was placed at the centre of the remains of the back wall where the firegrate had been. It states

"The site of the Old School" and underneath in brackets "The Hearse House."

Thus, a long, as yet undocumented, history of this small piece of land reached its sad but useful end.

"RULES AND REGULATIONS OF THE HEARSE
KEPT IN THE PARISH OF LAMPLUGH, 1900

1   The Committee of Management shall be chosen annually by the subscribers, consisting of four subscribers, one from each Township, and that one of the four shall be appointed Treasurer and Secretary, and also that each Committeeman shall be provided with a book wherein to enter the names of subscribers, and accounts relating to the hearse.

2   The committee shall appoint a Guardian to clean and take care of the Hearse, Harness, and Hearse Horse, and that he shall receive, for his services 1/6d each time the hearse is used.

3   That all monies received by the Committee, together with the balance in hand, shall be handed over to the Treasurer to form a fund to be expended in paying the Guardian's Fees, and in any repairs that may from time to time become necessary in the Hearse, Harness, or Hearse House, and that the said Committee, or a majority of them, shall have power to determine as to the necessity of such repairs and to order accordingly.

4   That the Hearse shall be the property of the subscribers, and that any person resident in the Parish of Lamplugh, or any non-resident owner of property in the said parish, shall become a subscriber on payment of Five Shillings, and shall be entitled to the same privileges as the original subscribers.

5   Each original subscriber, resident in the Parish of Lamplugh, shall be entitled to the use of the Hearse for himself, his wife and children, but not for other relatives, unless resident at his house, and at the death of such Subscriber and his widow, his children shall be entitled the use of the hearse, provided they reside in the said Parish, but at the death of such children the claim shall cease.

6   Any original subscriber who leaves the Parish of Lamplugh, or any non-resident owner of property in the said Parish, who is a subscriber, shall be entitled to the same privileges as if resident in the Parish, but at the death of such subscriber and his widow, the claim shall cease.

7   The fee to subscribers shall be Two Shillings and Sixpence, to non subscribers. Five shillings, if the Hearse is required to go out of the Parish; if not, Three Shillings for each funeral; and if the Hearse is required to attend a funeral to a distance about 8 miles from Lamplugh Cross, an extra fee of Sixpence per mile shall be charged for each mile, or fraction of a mile, above that distance.

8   All applications for the use of the Hearse shall be made to the Treasurer, or one of the Committee, who, on receipt of the fee, shall grant a written certificate, such certificate shall be delivered to the Guardian before any person shall be used in the order of application.

9   Every person using the Hearse shall return it to the Hearse house on the same day that it is taken out, and should any person deface, or damage the Hearse through carelessness, or wilful negligence, he shall repair it to the entire satisfaction of the Committee, or in default the Committee shall repair the Hearse, and charge the said defaulting party with costs thereof, to be recovered by distraint if necessary.

10   The Committee shall audit the accounts, and lay a statement thereof before a meeting of the subscribers, to be held annually on New Years Day, or the first convenient day after, in the Schoolroom, Lamplugh, for the purpose of appointing a Committee for the ensuing year, and transacting other business connected with the Hearse, and that the balance in hand after such meeting, shall be placed in the Savings Bank at Whitehaven, in the names of Treasurer and Secretary to the Lamplugh Hearse.

11   That should any case arrive which is not provided for in the above Rules, the Committee, or a majority of them shall have power to determine.

12   That no alteration shall be made in the above Rules, but at a General Meeting of the Subscribers, which shall be called by the Committee for that purpose.

John Rogers	Mill Gill Head
John Porter	Cockley Gill
Henry Mossop	Kelton Head
Joseph Bowman	Cockan
Jonathan Wood	Brook House, Guardian"

The above rules were agreed at a General meeting of the Subscribers, held in the Schoolroom, Lamplugh, on the 8th day of January 1870. (17)

References

10.	Dickinson R. F.	Red How Family papers
11.	May T.	The Victorian Undertaker, Shire Publications
12.	Bragg M.	Land of the Lakes, Secker & Warburg Ltd 1983
13.	May T.	The Victorian Undertaker, Shire Publications
14.	Rollinson W.	Life & tradition in the Lake District, Dalesman Books 1981
15.	Findler G.	Folk Lore of the Lakes County
16.	Bruce K.W & M.I	Wood Family papers Mill How
17.	Bruce K.W & M.I.	Wood Family papers Mill How

CHAPTER 4
THE CHURCHYARD

Churchyards are important for various reasons, not least of which is that they often retain significant information about the history of the church and its parishioners. Headstones, carvings, memorials, occupations and ancient yew trees are some examples. A churchyard can also be important for its historical and archaeological value along with its main role, which is that of a place for Christian burial. Like church buildings, churchyards have witnessed changes and adaptations over the last thousand years to meet the needs of their congregations. The church and churchyards provide a strong physical and emotional link with the past. Some can hold fascinating stories. The burial ground can give clues about traditions and the communities that have created and maintained them. The care of large churchyards such as Lamplugh can be an onerous task. At present one person, Cyril Atkinson, carries out neat and caring maintenance of the churchyard at Lamplugh. In times not too distant in the memory, "boon days" were held when a group of parishioners worked together to do this same maintenance.

Long before Christianity reached the shores of the United Kingdom, burial places certainly existed. Burial grounds had been used for many centuries as

> "communal and secular, no less than religious purposes, in an age when the two were essentially one and indivisible" (Mortimer Wheeler).

Research has discovered that there are many churchyards older than the building or buildings within them. This is the case at St Michael's. The Celts frequently surrounded their church with a wall or a raised embankment. Originally many churchyards were circular in shape. It is only from Saxon times that the churchyards became rectangular. In Saxon times pagan sites were still being used for burial as well as being used for their general assemblies and moot courts. Burials mostly took place on the south side of the church and festivities and meetings on the north side. A raised churchyard can sometimes be, and often is, an indication of a church's antiquity, a result of the constant re-use of the same piece of land for burials over the centuries. Over time the practice of reusing ground in this way naturally and inevitably raises the level of soil well above that of the adjoining land. This could appear to be a possibility at St Michaels, as the height of the ground within the enclosing wall differs greatly from the road level and the land adjacent belonging to Lamplugh Hall. On the opposite northern side the ground is certainly much lower and nearer the height of the surrounding fields.

Until the 18th century, corpses were buried not in wooden coffins, but bound in cloth. Many parishes kept a special coffin in which the corpse was carried only during the service and there is no reason to suppose that Lamplugh was any different in this respect. The 'uncoffined' and therefore corpses wrapped in cloth (Burial in Wool Act, 1678, re church registers) were put in the ground, one on top of the other, in the south side of the churchyard.

MEMORIALS AND HEADSTONES

The gentry of a parish were invariably interred inside their parish church. Lamplugh is no exception. The chancel and vestry was once the private chapel of the Lamplugh family. The flags in the chancel were raised to enable a burial to take place. Today there are few visible ancient or memorial gravestones of members of the Lamplugh family in the church or present churchyard. The oldest stone of the Lamplugh family is said to belong to a member of the family who took part in the Crusades. The stone can be found outside to the left of the War Memorial, near the guard railings. It is believed that originally the gravestone was at one time inside the church, but for some reason that has been lost in the mists of time, it was placed where it lies now and not returned to its original resting place. It is possible it could have been moved at the same time as the headstone of John Lamplugh was taken from the chancel and placed in the vestry. This possibly could have occurred during one of the alterations to the church building. The antiquity of the crusader stone makes decay inevitable; it has been exposed to the elements over a prolonged time; it has deteriorated quite markedly over the last thirty years. It had certainly been well protected at the start of its life. On looking closer at the photograph there is a suggestion of a shape of the human form. Could this have been a brass effigy that was removed before it was placed in the churchyard? The writing and marks are now almost indecipherable.

The 'John Lamplugh' stone to be found in the vestry is dated 1634. The tombstone is now fixed on the west wall of the vestry, but it was formerly on the south side of the altar table. The inscription is written in Latin. A translation is as follows:

> "Here lies John Lamplugh Esqre. Gentleman of ancient family, patron of this church, who died March 24th age 48. He took to wife Elizabeth, daughter of Sir Edward Musgrave at Hayton and they were parents of twelve children. I believe that the day cometh when happy I shall rise again, Christ alone is my sure salvation."

There are also the memorials of the Brisco branch of the Lamplugh family high on the west walls of the church. There are some tombstones of more recent Brooksbank descendants of the Lamplugh family, to be found in the northwest of the churchyard. The Dickinson family, who over the centuries served as Squires to the Lamplugh family, have family headstones of their ancestors in the churchyard.

The family has lived continuously in Lamplugh at Streetgate, Havercroft and Red How over many centuries. One memorial of this family is placed in what was the old choir doorway and has the family coat of arms at the top. There are also memorial windows and plaques in the church dedicated to more recent members of this family. The last member of the Dickinson family to be buried at Lamplugh was Ronald Fryer Dickinson in 1985. His tombstone states he was "a Justice of the Peace, an accomplished artist and was High Sheriff of Cumberland" in 1953, the year of the Coronation of Elizabeth II. He then served as Deputy Lieutenant of Cumbria for many years. He was also a knowledgeable historian and left personal and family notes and numerous manuscripts, many of which have been referred to in this book. The Rogers family, who at one time lived at Greensyke, donated stained glass windows in memory of members of

The crusader stone photographed circa 1950

The old choir doorway

41

their family. They have many descendants living in New Zealand who return quite often to visit the churchyard seeking out the family tombstones.

The present tombstones in the churchyard have been recorded, a fully detailed survey being made in 1993/94. This was carried out under the leadership of Maureen Fisher and Ian Smith. The results have been deposited with the present vicar, Rev. Peter J Simpson, Ennerdale, in the archives of Lamplugh & District Heritage Society and the Local Record Office at Whitehaven.

The survey discovered that

> "the present number of tombstones did not remotely reflect the number of burials recorded in the Parish Registers even though many graves were found to have no identifications. These unidentified burial mounds were also recorded." (18)

This fact supports the theory of the raised level of the burial ground previously mentioned. Further evidence of unmarked graves, based on research, shows that at least thirteen of the Parish Rectors are recorded in the registers as having been buried at St Michael's. Headstones mark the resting-place of only five of them. All those marked are dated 1729 and afterwards. These are, David King, Clement Nicholson, Joseph Gilbanks, Richard Haythornthwaite and Leslie Arthur Goddard. The reading of David King's headstone can be puzzling. The secret is to read it as if it were the pages of an open book. The Rev Percy Parminter on his retirement came to live at Lingcroft when he undertook to be the temporary priest in charge during an unusually long interregnum before the arrival of the Rev Claude T. Shuttleworth. He is not named in official records but is buried in the churchyard near the Rev Richard Haythornthwaite.

In the late 17th century the affluent yeoman farmers and master tradesmen felt the need to commission memorial headstones to be erected in a similar way to the gentry, at the churchyard graves of their ancestors. Thus the placing of headstones, as we know them now, began as a 17th century fashion. Most gravestones in St Michael's churchyard date from the 18th century or later. Many headstones have biblical quotations and interesting carvings. There are only a few epitaphs. The one for John Bowman 1798 reads:

> "The family all to this dark tomb are gone
> And we who live must follow everyone.
> What fate commands, frail nature must obey
> How short the time that we can have to stay."

Some members of the 'old families' of Lamplugh emigrated and so died abroad, but in some instances their names have been recorded on the family tombstones in Lamplugh churchyard. Some younger sons became mariners at the time when Whitehaven was at the height of its trading with the Americas. The locations mentioned on tombstones include New Zealand, Australia including Tasmania, Jamaica, Canada, South Africa and Jerusalem.

Some emigrants took the name Lamplugh with them to the Upper Plenty area of Victoria, in Australia. William Nicholson of Lane Foot, Lamplugh, born 1791, spade maker, and his son Anthony, born circa 1816 eventually settled on a bank of the Plenty River near Whittlesea, a wheat growing area just north of Melbourne. Their farmhouse 'Lamplough Hall,' at one time the most important home in the district, is now a ruin. James Coulthard of Cockan, Lamplugh, born 1840 arrived at Whittlesea, Victoria, on the 'Commodore Perry' in 1863. He built a home 'Wildwood' close to 'Lamplough Hall'. The two families eventually intermarried and descendants retain long but distant connections with Lamplugh. Graves of the old established families of Lamplugh can be found in 'clutches'. It would appear that at one time the burials were made in related family groups.

Gravestones of special interest that once stood in the 'old Parsonage area' were of German soldiers who had died in a flu epidemic whilst they were imprisoned in the POW Camp in Lamplugh during the First World War. The prison camp was by the Coast to Coast cycleway between Salter and Rowrah Hall. The bodies have now been exhumed and removed to a German war cemetery at Cannock Chase in Staffordshire.

Some tombstones face downwards close to the northern side of the church walls and were placed there during the last re building of the church to be near as possible to their original position. The story of the Dickinson memorial stone being placed in the old choir doorway and the headstones facing downwards nearby, can be found in the George Dickinson jottings on page 50.

Genealogy today is a fast growing hobby. The recording of all the headstones has created a vital source of information as well as interest. Names of relatives are frequently requested now, so this survey will surely be of increasing value to future researchers and historians.

THE ENVIRONMENT

As far as anyone knows, there has been little research into the environment of the churchyard other than lichens. A study of the history of many of the trees and the variety of wildlife and flowers has yet to be undertaken. Snowdrops, crocuses and daffodils grow in the older areas of the churchyard. Pagans grew snowdrops on what are now old ecclesiastical sites. Their appearance in February signified the awakening of the land and the growing power of the Sun. In early Christian times, February 2nd was dedicated to the Purification of the blessed Virgin Mary, when mothers carried lighted candles when taking their children, born during the preceding year, to church. It became known as Candlemas. This is an example of the substitution by the early church of a Christian ceremony for a pagan festival. An old folk saying states

"By Candlemas day all geese should lay
And all good hogs do without hay."

The Mothers' Union marked the millennium by planting a cherry tree. This can be found near the main doorway and is now marked with a small plaque.

Yew trees are renowned for their longevity and mystical power. In fact the oldest wooden weapons yet discovered were made of yew. Yews are most certainly associated with ancestral burial grounds. Recent research suggests that Bronze Age barrows were surrounded with yews. Stuart Friar in his book about Parish Churches states

"that it cannot be by chance that one of the letters of the runic alphabet is also the English name for yew."

One legend says that yew trees provided shelter for the first Christian missionaries that arrived in this country and so were planted in churchyards as a reminder. Another legend says that they were planted in churchyards because at one time archery practice took place there and the churchyard yews provided the raw material for the bowmen to make the English longbow. Whilst this was debatable, there is no doubt that in 1307, Edward I ordered that yews should be planted in churchyards. This was allegedly to protect the buildings from high winds and storms. Palm Sunday was known as Yew Sunday in medieval times. There are several old yews in the Lamplugh churchyard. It is very difficult to discover the exact age of a yew tree and so their ages remain a mystery.

Old Yew trees in Lamplugh church yard.

War memorial in its original position

THE WAR MEMORIAL

The war memorial commemorating the parishioners who gave their lives in World War I was unveiled and consecrated at a special ceremony held in June 1921. The clergy taking part were: - The Bishop of Carlisle, Rev Basil Sherwen the Rector of Dean plus Rev R. Haythornthwaite, Rector of Lamplugh. There was a large congregation which included many relatives of the fallen. So many people attended the ceremony that many were unable to gain admission into the church.

After the first part of the service, which was held in the church, everyone moved outside to witness the consecration and unveiling. Colonel D. J. Mason D.S.O. addressed the entire assembled congregation. Amongst other things he reminded the people

"of the high tradition of their own parish and that these men we laurel today kept the shield of England bright by that same spirit of self sacrifice which has inspired ' the lang, lean men of Lampla' for eight hundred years."(19)

A historian of the Middle Ages had said,

"There lives in Lamplugh a race of valorous gentlemen successively for their worthiness knighted in the field, all, or the most part of them. Thank God, the spirit of those Lamplugh's, who by personal bravery won the gilt spurs of knighthood during five hundred years of the early history of Old England, still remains in those who, as this great world spins down the ringing grooves of change, now people this countryside."

After his address he unveiled the monument, a description of which was given in a local paper at the time, as follows:

"The war memorial is a runic cross of grey granite, and occupies a prominent position under the west window of the church. At the base of the cross are the words, 'There was war in heaven; Michael and his angels fought against the dragon.'"

The cross stands on a pedestal on the front of which is the inscription:

"In proud and grateful memory of the sons of this parish, who, when there was war on earth (1914 – 1918) fought against evil and gave their lives, but their cause prevailed"

On the sides are inscribed the names of all the fallen and the upper base reads

"Their name liveth for evermore."

On the lower base is carved in relief a sheathed sword. The report also adds that

"the spaces on each side of the monument had been neatly enclosed with a boxwood border and planted with forget-me-nots by Mr. Fawcett, gardener at Red How."

"After the consecration by the Bishop, Bugler I. Beck, 5th Border Regiment sounded the 'Last Post.' To close the ceremony the choir sung the hymn of sacrifice "O valiant hearts; who to your glory came." The service concluded, the mourners then placed their own personal tributes at the foot of the monument."

The War Memorial was erected by public subscription and the local committee overseeing the organisation and placing at Lamplugh was Messrs. Geo. Dickinson, Chairman, Red How; H. Smith, Kelton Head; J. R. Tinnion, Greensyke; Jos. Wood, Brook House; Rev R. Haythornthwaite, Treasurer, Lamplugh Rectory; and Francis Stephens, Fell Dyke, Secretary. Messrs. Beattie and Co, Carlisle supplied the monument.

The war memorial was moved from its place next to the wall under the west window to its present position when the names of the men of the parish who paid 'the supreme sacrifice' during World War II were added. It was also rotated 180 degrees so that its front faced the church. (19) Plans are in place for cleaning and repainting the lettering on the War memorial during 2004.

THE CHURCH BELLS

From medieval times, throughout the land a bell or bells of a church summoned people to worship. In past times they were also rung at the time the parson or rector said his own offices. For many people the bells were their only means of telling the time of day and passage of time other than from the position of the sun. Parishioners knew at what time they were rung and for what purpose. Most medieval churches are said to have possessed a sundial on the south wall to show the passage of time. No sundial has been recorded at St Michael's but there is an ancient dial set into the wall on the south side of Lamplugh Hall gates. Was one used in Lamplugh? Could it originally have been placed on the church?

The old sundial

Medieval bells tolled a curfew and in some instances bells rang when there was danger of invasion as in World War II. They also announced the death of a parishioner. Traditionally country wide it was three times three for a male and two times three for a female followed by the number in years of the dead person's age.

"In Troutbeck the 'passing bell' tolled nine times for a man, six times for a woman, and three times for a child." (20)

What the sequence of numbers that were rung at Lamplugh is not known, there is no recorded proof, but it is certain that the bells were tolled and still are at set intervals for the dead.

At the time when the Border Reivers were raiding in these parts, it is probable that an agreed signal using the bells would have been used as a method of communicating to the people that there was imminent danger. During the Reformation, an order was made for church bells to be taken down and destroyed. Many church bells were silenced and/or removed but the bells at St Michael's must have been saved or kept in safety somewhere.

The bells were taken down in 1951 for repairs to the bell turret. It was discovered that one was a good example of a 15th century bell. This was interesting as no known record existed. The bell was thought to be the work of famous bell founders of York. It was also found to be still in good condition and still retained its tone. Only minor work was considered necessary before it was re-hung.

"The bell measured 21½ inches in diameter at mouth and was 16½ inches high; the inscription round its shoulder within quadruple bands has a small initial cross, followed by "THOMAS LAMPLO MILES ANIMA MEA BEATA" and closes with an upright arrow and X barred above and below; there are no interval stops. Below the lower bands is an armorial shield surmounted by a royal crown; the armorial is that of the Kings of England, as used from c. 1320 until the middle of the 15th century: fleurs de lys 2 and 1, one and four; lions regardent 1,2,3,two and three. Following this, not in an inscription band, on separate paterae, are the letters OBEIVS. Scattered low down on the body of the bell, come several damaged and mainly illegible Lombardic letters; one of them is a T, possibly a founders mark, for it occurs on the sound bow of the two bells at St Bridget's, Beckermet. The letters are Lombardic of late character, with A given upside down and S reversed".

The 15th century Church Bell

"Sir Thomas Lamplugh is recorded as from 1460 –1471; he was High Sheriff of Cumberland. The bell may thus be securely dated to the third quarter of the 15th century."(21)

The second bell is more recent and is probably Victorian, a 19th Century replacement for an earlier one. For those interested, it is possible to see some of the inscription through a good camera lens or a pair of binoculars. It is also worth noting the beautiful cross carved within a circle, which enhances the turret below the spire. In the previous church, the bell turret was placed in the middle of the building and the ropes hung down and were tied to the side of the three decker pulpit.

THE WEATHERVANE

A weathervane needs to be free to be able to revolve easily to show the wind direction. Cockerels used in past ages symbolised vigilance but more importantly their tails, which are usually prominent, showed the wind direction. Use of a cockerel as a weathercock has been popular for many centuries. The Bayeux Tapestry, embroidered during the 11th century after the Battle of Hastings, shows that they were in use at that time. It would seem probable that the idea or tradition might have originated in France and been introduced here after the Conquest. The cockerel was one of the emblems of the French nation for centuries. Originally, coats of arms of the donors were painted on the sides of the cockerel, but during Victorian times weathercocks, which were often of a Gothic design, were rarely painted.

The weathercock at St Michael's, Lamplugh sits on the top of the bell turret, which is the highest part of the building. Its tail is elongated. At what date a weathercock was originally placed on the present church is not known exactly, but it was after the 1870 reconstruction, as the previous church only had a carved sandstone cross on the top of the bell turret. The weathercock has suffered from the buffeting of the winds and rain that it has to encounter. It was damaged during a lightning storm and was repaired and replaced in the 1990s.

References

18. Fisher, M. & Smith I.   Lamplugh Churchyard notes 1994
19. West Cumberland Times Newspaper clipping dated 22, 06, 1921
20. Bragg, M.   Land of the Lakes, Secker & Warburg Ltd, 1983
21. Fair, M. C.   C&WAA S Vol. L, New Series, 1951

CHAPTER 5
RECONSTRUCTIONS OF THE CHURCH

The earliest records of any reconstruction of St Michael's were in 1658. The church up until this time was still thatched either with straw or heather and most probably had been built by the parishioners themselves. It was probably at that time that the leaded roof referred to in 1771 was put in place. There had been a lead roof on the chancel, but there was a letter from the parson urging that slates be put on in its place, as the lead was very old and letting in the rain. The last major reconstruction of the church as it now stands, was in 1869-70. During 2003 the church roof was stripped and re-slated, making use of the original Lake District slate, and the interior has been redecorated. Updating is planned for the lighting and heating systems.

The first written reference to the 1658 reconstruction is to be found in the parish register, which reads;

> "Memorand: That this yeare above written the pishe Church of this Lamplugh was growne in such ruine and decay both in timber and walles that pishioners was glad to take all the tymber downe and most of the walles and build it up again upon their charges, it being soe good a work I thought good for my credit and the satisfaction of those who knowes not the same to register it 1658. Pickering Hewer."

Pickering Hewer is described as a Curate and it is possible that Cromwells Puritans turned out John Braithwaite (Parson), during the Commonwealth, after the execution of Charles I in 1649 and before the Restoration of Charles II in 1660.

The Churchwardens' Account book referring to the 1771 church alterations, notes that

> 'The total cost to the parishioners was £67.2s.10d." (Today £67.15p)

This fact is also recorded as a Memorandum in the Parish Registers, but on a page devoted to records dated 1734. The explanation given is:

> "placed there because there was room for the entry"

> "Lamplugh Church flagged back'd seats pulpit in the middle of Church five new windows, ceil'd overhead, placed in this old register because here was room to transmit it to posterity this year 1771."

An added entry also states:

> "It was with great difficulty that the church was repaired in the year 1771 that year being very remarkable for oppositions in this Parish, pride and ignorance being there in conjunction".

An extract from a letter amongst the Dickinson papers 'The Chancel Roof – repairs' and dated 1768 gives a different point of view:

Letter from Richard Dickinson to T. L. 15th August 1768

"The chancel hath been covered with lead, but Mr Jefferson was imposed upon by the workmen who did it, for the lead is so very thin that it hath been insufficient to keep out the rain for thirty years past. The timber by being kept continually wet, in the winter season, is greatly decay'd. So that there is a necessity for a new Roof. As the Body of the Church is covered with blue Slate, and also a part of the Chancel which is appropriated or set apart as a Burial place for the Family of Lamplugh Hall, and hath been slated at their Expence: Mr Lucock, the Acting Trustee proposes to take this trouble upon himself, and also to put a good and sufficient covering of the best blue slate upon the Chancel, with good sound timber, and all things requisite.

The parishioners advise us to take this method: They think that a covering of the best blue slates is a dryer and better covering than with lead, which is continually wanting repairs.

Alterations of this kind are frequent in the neighbouring Parishes. At Bridekirk the Church and Chancel were both covered with lead, but complaints being often made of the insufficiency of the roof; it was agreed to take off the lead and cover them as they are at present, with blue slate, and in the parish of Brigham as I am informed they are going to do the same."(22)

GEORGE DICKINSON'S JOTTINGS

The reconstructed Church of 1771 has been described in some of the jottings of George Dickinson, Red How. (23)

" The old Nave was pulled down in 1869 and rebuilt as at present. There is a picture of the old church in the Billiard room here. In the old church the pulpit was a three decker:- that is a little pew at the bottom for the Parish Clerk, then the reading desk above, and above all the pulpit. It was in the middle of the arch and on the steps leading up to the chancel and there were two pews only in the chancel, the Streetgate pew on the North side and the Lamplughs' pew on the South side. The first Rector that I remember was Walter Brooksbank - he read the service in a white gown but before the sermon went into the passage behind the pulpit that is between the two pews above mentioned and put on the black gown in which he preached.

The bell or bells, I forget if there was more than one, were hung outside above the archway and the rope came down to the steps where the Clerk rang the bell and then hung up the rope on to the side of the pulpit. The pews in those days were all closed in with doors and the Red How Pew was the pew nearest the door on the south side. It has a curtain of red mohair at the back to keep the draught off our heads. There were seats on both sides so that as elsewhere we sat facing and back to the clergyman. The main door did not come in at the end of the Church as it does now; there was a gallery of three or four rows of pews between the entrance and the west window with passage up the middle. The Sunday scholars and schoolmaster used to sit in one of these pews and one Sunday during the sermon there was a crash and the schoolmaster and all the boys had disappeared, the seat had given way and they were all scrambling on the floor. The Parson Brooksbank was a very humorous man and burst out laughing in the pulpit. There was no choir, the whole congregation singing being led by the Parish Clerk who also read the responses in a very loud voice. There was no organ or harmonium and the Clerk struck the note with a tuning fork. Upon one occasion after striking the note he shouted out, "nea that's ower hea" and struck it again on a lower note.

When the railway here was made, the stationmaster High became a regular attendant at Lamplugh Church. He had also been a Parish Clerk and repeated the responses in a very loud voice, much to the disgust of our own Parish Clerk, the competition between them causing great amusement to us children. On each side of the altar, before the alterations, was a big blackboard, on the one were the names of rectors and on the other the Ten Commandments or the Lord's Prayer, I forget which.

When the Nave of the church was rebuilt it was somewhat widened, and during the operations when my father went up to see what was going on he found that they were digging foundations for the new walls over some of the graves of our ancestors and there were some of the bones cut. He was furious and had them all put back at once threatening to stop the whole work as it had begun before the faculty was actually granted. He was afraid, however that some of the bones had already been dug up and reburied in a common grave near the wall on the east side of the church yard between Lamplugh Hall gateway and where the gas how* now stands. An old family tombstone (this was commissioned by John Dickinson of Streetgate in June 1760, at a cost of 6 guineas (£6. 30p)) on which was our coat of arms, had to be removed and it was arranged that father should have a new tombstone cut and it was then placed in the old choir doorway upon the other side of the chancel, the doorway being then closed up."

At the time of an undated, but possibly the 1870 reconstruction, Mr Ronald F. Dickinson has made a note that:

"Beneath the plaster in the Vestry, within the South Wall was found a shallow stone arch approximately four and a half feet wide over a built up 'niche', the lower part of which remained below present floor level. Possibly a tomb, in view of the known fact that this part of the building was formerly reserved as 'a burial place for the Lamplugh family.' " (23a)

* *The gas how was a tall wooden construction that stood near the stone shed at the rear entrance to the church. It was a cover for the machinery that worked the gas lighting system inside of the church. Some visitors once asked what it was and a local farmer told them that the village once kept a giraffe and this was where it was buried!*

References

22.	Dickinson Rev R.	Dickinson Red How, Family papers
??	Dickinson, G.	Dickinson Red How, Family papers
23a.	Dickinson. R.F.	Dickinson Red How, Family papers

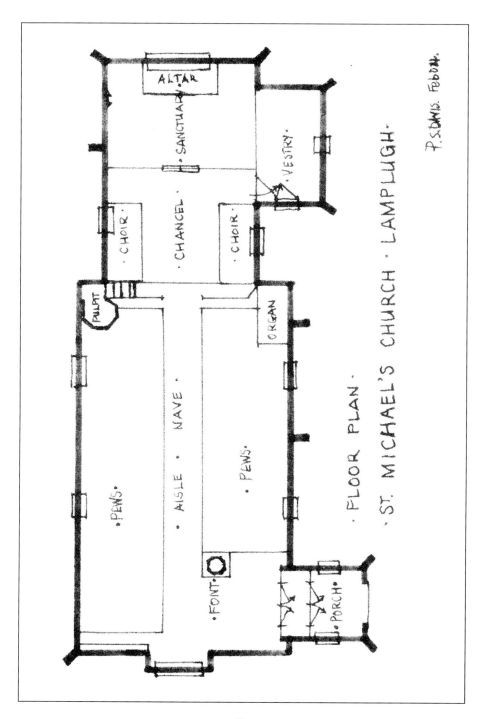

ALTAR

· SANCTUARY ·

· CHANCEL ·

CHOIR ·

CHOIR ·

VESTRY ·

PULPIT

ORGAN

· NAVE ·

· AISLE ·

· PEWS ·

· PEWS ·

· PEWS ·

· FONT ·

· PORCH ·

· FLOOR PLAN ·

· ST. MICHAEL'S CHURCH · LAMPLUGH ·

P.S.DAVIS. Feb.04.

52

CHAPTER 6
THE CHURCH TODAY

BUILDING OF THE PRESENT CHURCH

In 1869 James Lamplugh Raper, the then Lord of the Manor, left £2,000 to do 'further reconstruction.' The contractor was John Youart of St. Bees and whilst the rebuilding was taking place the services were held in the school. The school referred to is Lamplugh Parochial School, which was by then the new school next to the Lamplugh W. I. This school closed in 1951 and some years later was reconstructed into the house named 'Dhustone.' The original school boundary walls still surround the property.

A faculty for demolition of the church, dated July 1869, was granted to Walter Brooksbank, the Rector, John Rogers and Daniel Rogers, who were churchwardens, and Rev George Henry Ainger, D.D., to take down and remove the whole of the nave and porch, and also the chancel and the south chapel (now the vestry), except the two arches and part of the walling;

> "which is intended to retain and repair and to make use of the materials in the erection of the proposed new church according to the plans deposited in the Registry of Consistory Courts of Carlisle."

The design for the reconstruction of the church in 1870 was by the famous Victorian architect **William Butterfield. (1814-1900)**. Butterfield was born in London and worked for a London builder before serving an apprenticeship with an architect in Worcester. He set up his own practice in 1840. He was awarded the RIBA Gold medal in 1884 and became one of the most important and eminent Victorian Gothic architects of the time, and was noted for his liking of contrasting patterns in different colours. Nearly all his work was ecclesiastical.

St Michael's Church, Lamplugh, is the only example of a church in Cumberland completely designed by him. He was involved with some restoration work at St. Bega's Priory, St Bees in 1855 and St. Bridget's Church, Brigham in 1864. This important ecclesiastical architect, created many other churches and chapels, which included Rugby School Chapel, Keble College Chapel and Balliol College Chapel, Oxford. He was especially famous for being the architect for All Saints Church, Margaret Street, near Oxford Circus in London. He also designed St Ninian's Cathedral in Perth, Scotland and the Anglican Cathedral in Melbourne, Australia amongst many others.

The Church interior 1970

Bishops chair at a recent Flower Festival.

THE CHANCEL

In the chancel of the old church was placed the Lamplugh family vault, which was at one time surmounted by two elaborately carved marble monuments to the members of that family. These can now be seen on the west wall of the present church. That on the south side commemorates Thomas Lamplugh, Frances his wife, and their son-in-law, Richard Brisco, all from the middle of the 18th century.

The inscriptions are as follows:

The inscription on the north side of the window bears the arms of Brisco impaling those of Lamplugh and a medallion of a lady's head and also these words:

"Sacred to the memory
Of
Thomas Lamplugh. Esqre., and Frances
His wife
Who sleep below.
The former died aged 81
The latter 5th January 1745
Aged 80.
This monument likewise preserved the memory of
Ricd Brisco, Esqre., eldest s. of
Jno Brisco of Crofton Esq.
Their son in law, who in duty, affection
And gratitude, by his wife appointed this
memorial to them. He died 26th January 1750 aged 54.
His friendship was open, sincere and zealous.
As a neighbour he studied to be useful
In prudent hospitality seldom equal'd
In him ye poor found compassionate relief
To lament and admire are not so valuable
As to imitate."

" Here lyeth the body of
Mrs. Margaret Brisco.
Descended from an ancient and honourable family.
A dutiful child, sincere friend, and loving wife.
who was mistress of all the Graces that
adorn the female mind,
Modest, chaste, and prudent,
Temperate, affable, courteous,
Charitable to the poor, benevolent to all;
Thus blessed with so many valuable qualities,
rare and uncommon to be found in one and
the same person, she gained the esteem and
admiration of all who knew her
excepting only those
whose envy made them repine at her virtues,
in so much that she was equalled by very few,
surpassed by none of her time.
How dear her memory is to her husband
and parents let this monument show,
erected by their pious care,
And a faint image of their lasting grief.
She was Daughter to Thomas Lamplugh,
Esq. and Frances his wife, of Lamplugh,
Born October 7th 1693
Married to Mr. Richard Brisco, son and heir
Of John Brisco, Esqr, of Crofton, in the
year 1731, and died July 21st of the same year."

THE ALTAR

In Britain most Celtic churches from the beginning of the 6th century had used stone to erect an altar. The term altar to be accurate should only be applied to medieval stone altars though it is commonly used also to describe Post-Reformation communion tables. The altar at St Michael's is made of stone with carvings around it. It is old but how old is not really known. An altar tabletop of stone is an unusual feature in a church. The front and the sides of the altar are made out of carved wood with some painted panels and covered with a decorative altar frontal. An act of Edward VI (1547 - 53) stated that all altars made of stone were to be removed and destroyed as they were considered to be pagan. In many cases they were hidden in anticipation of better times. It is quite possible that someone covered this stone altar with wood or it was hidden away until the danger of the altar being taken and destroyed was past. A few have been found intact in Celtic and Anglo-Saxon churches and restored. Butterworth integrated into his plans the old stone altar with its carvings when he redesigned the church in 1870. The old wooden altar table now standing inside the main entrance on the left is inscribed

" The gift of Mrs. Frances Lamplugh March 16th 1737".

The old wooden altar table

56

It was used as the altar table from 1737 until the reconstruction of 1870.

At the present time the church possesses four altar frontals. The families of Jane Sophia Whitten and Cecily Sharpe gave one each in memory of their mothers. There is a plain linen frontal which was made by Mrs. Shuttleworth, whilst her husband was the rector, for use during Lent. The most elaborate and intricate one is the oldest and was sewn and hand embroidered with silks and gold thread by Miss Brooksbank, a Lamplugh family descendant, whilst she was living in London through the 'Blitz' during the Second World War. It was presented to the church shortly after this event. Until the 1960s this was the only frontal that existed in the church.

Curtains at the side of the altar cover a traditional Victorian zigzag tile decoration, very much in vogue during the late 19th century. The curtain material was bought from donations made by various parishioners and sewn prior to the centenary celebrations in 1970. The red carpet was a replacement for a well-used, brown, corded, jute carpet. Fund raising for the new carpet being led and organised by three parishioners Mrs M. Carr, Mrs H. Rutherford and Mrs M.A. Stephens.

There are two chairs, one either side of the altar for the use of visiting bishops and clergy when taking part in special services. They are of differing styles. One is made from black bog oak and has carvings of oak leaves and acorns within a square twist on the backrest. In the centre of the square are the initials "J B" and underneath is the date 1852. The chair has a twisted bar across the front just underneath the seat and casters on each of the plain crossed legs. Was this given in memory of a member of the Lamplugh Brooksbank family? There are no records to be found as yet to confirm who J B was. The other chair is made of oak. On the centre back is a square carved panel on which the words "Praise ye the Lord" and "IHS" are written. It is carved with curving oak leaves and twirls. Protruding from the chair back are three points, each shaped in the form of a bishop's mitre. This is the chair reserved for and used by the Bishop and other important clergy who visit and take part in the church services.

Altar crosses and candlesticks were rarely used in churches until the 19th century. The candlesticks and the original Lamplugh Church altar cross, the one set with polished decorative stones, stand on the altar. The plain altar cross came to the church when the old Trinity Church in Whitehaven was closed and its various possessions were distributed to the churches in the Deanery. (At the time Rev A.W. Binns was rector.) This usually stands on top of the hymnal shelf under the west window. The stainless steel altar vases, which are hand beaten, were made at the Industrial School of Art in Keswick. They were presented to the Church at the Centenary Service, 1970, in memory of the Rogers family, two members being present when the Bishop blessed and dedicated them. The family ancestors had previously donated stained glass windows.

Near the screen within the rails of the altar stands an oak side/serving table made by William Sewell of Fell Dyke, also a local craftsman. It is dedicated to the memory of his late wife, Mary Lizzie Sewell, and dated 1962.

There are two sets of Church Plate. One chalice is made of very old Cumberland silver one of the few remaining examples of its kind in Cumbria. The maker's mark is known in London and also on the Continent. However the chalice is rare in having survived the destruction at the time of the Commonwealth. It was probably hidden in Lamplugh Hall at the time. It is now used only on special occasions such as Easter and Christmas and is kept the rest of the year in a bank vault. The second set, bought with the legacy of and in memory of a parishioner, Minnie Sisson of Mill Gill Head Cottage is much smaller and is the one in regular use. There was until recently a beautiful, large, brass, hand beaten alms dish on which were designs of vines with grapes, but this was stolen. John B. Stalker presented a candlesnuffer to the church; previous to this, 'blowing of the breath' or 'pinching with fingers' was the only means of putting out the altar candles.

Until recently two plain simple stools stood on each side of the altar. These were for placing in the chancel at the time of a funeral. They are called coffin stools simply because the coffin was placed on them before and during a burial service as the old bier had no legs. This type of stool was at one time quite common but now is quite rare. These were used at every funeral up until 1970 when John B. Stalker, Clerk, donated a folding bier with wheels, which has been used ever since. The stools are now used for flower displays.

THE VESTRY

The oldest part of the church still standing is the vestry. The most interesting part is one of its windows. Its depth can be seen on the inside, but on the outside of the stone surround there are two small, carved faces to be seen. The window and carvings are said to be 15th century. The vestry at one time belonged to the descendants of the Lamplughs and was probably the mortuary chapel or part of it. George Dickinson's Jottings, 1828, states that at that time the vestry still belonged to the descendants of the Lamplughs.

15th century window.

58

In 2001, the present direct descendant of the Lamplugh family sold the titles of the Lords of the Manor of Lamplugh and Murton to two different people. This ended a connection with the Lamplugh family and possibly the church, that had been continuous for over 900 years. Whether there were any rights to/or about the vestry still belonging to the Lamplughs included in the sale, at this or at a previous time is not known.

The oak screen in the vestry was erected and dedicated

> "To the Glory of God and the memory of our beloved parents Richard Haythornthwaite Rector of Lamplugh 1909 - 1942 and Margaret Louisa Alston Haythornthwaite his wife. They loved this church."

It was made and carved by local joiner Henry Nevinson. He had helped to make the lych gates when he was an apprentice.

A clasped bible to be found in the vestry states that

> "James Sewell was the first child baptized in the new church August 28th 1870. Jas. Hacon, Rector."

On the flyleaf is the quote from Proverbs 22:6; 'Train up a child in the way he should go, and when he is old, he will not depart from it.'

THE WINDOWS

All the windows in the church are made of stained glass with the exception of the three plain leaded ones in the vestry. The large east window has three lights. The cost of this window was raised by subscription from the inhabitants and friends of the parish in 1882 and cost £102-10s-0d, James Macarthur was then the Rector. Along the bottom of the window, this information is incorporated for all to see. The three lights combine to depict the crucifixion of Christ. The crucifixion is in the centre light, and the two sidelights depict the two thieves and the group that stood round the Cross on that day. The writing on the window reads:

> "Jesus that he might sanctify the people with his new blood suffered without the gate"

There are three fine examples of windows designed by **Charles Eamer Kempe** and one other attributed to him, two in the chancel, the large west window and one in the nave. They are the work of Kempe and his company. They were commissioned and placed in the church between 1891 and 1911 by the Dickinson family of Red How.

1. "To the memory of Edward Harriman Dickinson born in mdcccxliii, grandson of Joseph Dickinson of Red How of this parish, Emma his wife dedicates this window."

The nave window designed by Charles Eamer Kempe depicting St Oswald and St Aidan.

The second window in the chancel attributed to Kempe is of the Madonna and Child. Some of his work went unsigned, the use of pearly edgings to garments (note the edge of the Madonna's cloak) and/or the addition of peacock feathers are acknowledged to be marks of his work. The dedication reads:

2. "To the glory of God and in loving memory of our parents John Dickinson 1810 – 1890. And Jane his wife 1816-1891 of Red How of this Parish "

In the nave the third window depicts St Oswald and St Aidan, its dedication reading:

3. "Giving thanks to God for the beloved memory of John Dickinson, his children have dedicated this window AD 1911".

The large west window represents St Michael and All Angels. 'St Michael and All Angels' is the church's official name and the principal archangel to whom the church is dedicated. St Michael has two other archangels by his side, they are Gabriel and Raphael. The writing on the dedication states:

4. "Giving thanks to God for the beloved memory of Joseph Dickinson of Red How. Mary his wife dedicates this window AD mcmx."

Charles Eamer Kempe (1837 - 1907) was an eminent Victorian stained glass artist and maker. He had wanted the Ministry to be his chosen career but recognised that, as he had a speech impediment, it would not be possible. After taking his Master's degree at Pembroke College, Oxford, he joined the firm of George F. Bodley, a successful Anglican architect, to study the architecture and decoration of churches. He studied medieval patterns in museums and manuscripts in churches. After designing church furniture he progressed to designing and the making of stained glass. Kempe stained glass was highly valued in his day. His style, it is claimed, though distinctive, was never quite original because his study of the patterns and the glass of northern Europe made in the fifteenth and early sixteenth century had influenced him greatly.

He began his own stained glass company, C. E. Kempe and Co in London in 1868. He perfected the use of silver stain on clear glass. It was in 1895 that his trade-mark became the wheat sheaf, taken from the Kempe family arms. His work can be found in twenty-seven British Cathedrals, some of these being Bristol, Gloucester, York, Winchester, Southwark, Lichfield and Hereford. He was also commissioned to produce a window of St George for Buckingham Palace. This window can now be seen in the museum of Ely Cathedral. One outstanding example of his firm's work in stained glass and church decoration is in the chancel of Sandringham Church in memory of King Edward VII and Queen Alexandra.

After his death his company carried on until 1934, but added a black tower to the sign of the wheat sheaf. Almost all his personal records and those of the firm were

Kempe trademark

destroyed after it closed down. Because of recent renewed interest in his work a 'Kempe Society' has been formed and holds a record of the stained glass he produced in the UK and Ireland. (24)

The three remaining windows were donated by the Rogers family of Greensyke and are to be found in the nave. They are as follows:

1. "In loving memory of Ann Braithwaite born 4 June 1862 and died 19 January 1865 and of John born March 1865 died 8 December 1865. This window is erected by their parents Daniel and Hannah Rogers of Greensyke."

2. "In memory of Daniel, Hannah and William Rogers of Greensyke MCMII."

The window is signed Heaton, Butler and Bayne, London** in the bottom right hand corner.

3. "In Memory of Annie Braithwate wife of William Rogers of Mill Gill Head born December 27 1788 died July 23 1858. Erected by her children. "

THE LECTERN

The word 'lectern' comes from the Latin word meaning 'to read' and the lectern's primary function is that of a reading stand. They were used in medieval times for the reading of the gospels and were placed in the chancel. In the 15th century hand-written books were so large and so heavy it was necessary to provide a lectern

Heaton, Butler and Bayne; *from 1860 - 1920, they were one of the most prosperous concerns who manufactured stained glass. The partners worked from 14 Garrick Street in Covent Garden and became London's foremost glass designers. All three partners were master craftsmen in their own right. This combination of skills produced some extremely creative stained glass to a high artistic standard. Their stained glass windows con be found all over the world. A rare chronicled video documentary called 'Stained Glass Masters' tells their story.*

to hold them. Following the Reformation, lecterns were replaced with reading desks located in the nave. The lessons at Matins and Evensong were read from them. In many instances they were incorporated in the middle 'deck' of a three decker pulpit. This was the case at St Michael's. George Dickinson in his jottings describes the Lamplugh three decker pulpit as it was before 1869. In the 1840s fashions had changed and many congregations followed the example of cathedrals and reintroduced separate lecterns. They were placed in the nave usually in front of the chancel arch. It was not until the new reconstruction in 1870 that Lamplugh had a brass eagle lectern.

When an eagle stands on an orb, then the orb represents the world. An outspread eagle standing on an orb is the symbol of St John the Evangelist whose words 'soared up into the presence of Christ' and so God's word would be carried across the world. The eagle was also known as the natural enemy of the serpent. The two outspread wings of the eagle were also a symbol to remind us that there are two different Testaments. The eagle lectern at Lamplugh has two outspread wings and stands on an orb. The Bible at present resting on the lectern and in common use is the one given by Ronald Dickinson and named "The Old and New Testament."

There are no ancient books existing in the church, but there are three large Books of Common Prayer, all of which are plainly bound with black leather. They were all in use regularly until the 1990s. One Book of Common Prayer is Victorian and shows the evidence of regular use, especially for Morning, Evening Prayer and the Litany. Many pieces of the pages and parts of the corners have been renewed and hand-written words have been added or glued over with newer details in the appropriate spaces. Names of Kings and Queens have been altered and the new names written in or stuck on top. A second Book of Common Prayer is labelled "Altar Services 1662 – 1928." The trustees of the Richard Brisco Scalesmoor Charity presented this book to Lamplugh Parish Church in 1963. It also includes the words of the Holy Communion service that was proposed in 1928. The third volume 'The Holy Bible,' presented to St Michael's by the Rev James K. Macarthur at Christmas 1884, stood on the eagle lectern for many years. The Altar Services book in present use, dated 14th October 1990 was presented by

> "Margaret and Tom Fullerton in memory of Thomas Jamieson, Churchwarden and Treasurer of the Parish of Lamplugh with Ennerdale (1964 -1989) and for many years Secretary and Verger of St. Michael's Lamplugh"

Near the lectern on the steps of the chancel stand two small boxes given in memory of Mabel Robinson, Streetgate. They originally contained a small shrub, but now are used for floral displays.

THE CHURCH ENTRANCE AND FONT

The Victorian sandstone font

The double oak inner doors were made by Henry Nevinson and were given in memory of John Ernest Douglas, High Park, (formerly of Lamplugh Hall) who died in 1964. It is a fitting memorial as he regularly sat near the back at the right hand side of the church and must frequently have felt the tremendous draught that used to penetrate through the outside doors. He served as a member of Lamplugh Parochial Church Council for many years.

Fonts in early churches were large basins, set below ground level in which a candidate for baptism was immersed. From the 11th and 12th century immersion was replaced by pouring of water over the head. Fonts were then raised above floor level. Some fonts were similar to a cup bowl. Saxon fonts resembled an upturned drum, were lined with lead, and stepped at the base.

The lead lining prevented the seepage of holy water left in the font to avoid the lengthy process of sanctification before each christening. Locked oak covers were added later to stop the use of this holy water for medical and other more sinister purposes.

The Victorian sandstone font with an oak cover which now stands inside the entrance into the present church was designed by Butterfield and placed there at the time of the 1870 reconstruction. A similar but older font can be seen standing outside of the church. There are also two plainer and roughly hewn ancient stone fonts, perhaps removed at the time of a former reconstruction. A brass ewer, which was used to carry water for christenings, stood on the steps of the font. It now leaks and is in need of repair.

THE ORGAN, ORGANISTS AND CHOIRS

The Willis pipe organ which is in use in the present church was originally built by the famous firm of Rushworth and Dreaper, Liverpool, and was presented to the church by Mr. George Dickinson of Red How in memory of his wife. A small brass plaque on the front of the instrument has the inscription

"To the glory of God and in gratitude for the best of wives."

The Lord Bishop of Carlisle dedicated the organ at a special service circa 1923. The Rev R. Haythornthwaite acted as Bishop's Chaplain. Mr. Charles Collins who had been chosen to be the organist for the occasion was a friend of Mr. George Dickinson and assistant organist of Liverpool Cathedral. He first of all played what was considered to be a most appropriate hymn "O praise ye the Lord." Following this he gave a recital which according to newspaper reports "showed the power and versatility of the instrument." (25)

The organ is a pipe organ with two manuals and foot pedals. There are five great stops, five swell stops, one pedal stop, and three couplers. It has been completely dismantled on two occasions to allow repairs. On one occasion it was mice chewing the leathers that were partly to blame for the damage. The last time it was completely dismantled was in 1997, when Thomas Pendlebury and Co. Ltd., Fleetwood, Lancashire completely stripped, rebuilt and made minor changes to the stops. When the original organ was installed a hand pump operated the bellows. A small corner adjacent to the organ was curtained off to hide the person who worked the pump during services. Mains electricity did not arrive in Lamplugh until the late 1950s, although just prior to that date the Parochial Church Council had invested in a generator in order to have electric lighting, which gave a brighter light and replaced the old hanging and standard gas lamps. A wooden box containing the electrical workings now occupies this site.

On top of this corner box now stands two challenge shields. They are almost one hundred years old and both were won outright by past Lamplugh Church Choirs. The larger of the two is the challenge shield of 'The Cumberland Musical Festival' (held at Workington) for adult church, chapel or mission choirs and was presented by the Rev Canon Rawnsley, a friend of Beatrix Potter and a founder of The National Trust. The Lamplugh Church Choir obtained the highest marks in this competition in three consecutive years to win the shield outright. The Junior Choir won the smaller of the two shields in 1906.

These choirs were trained and led by Charles Hales, the headmaster of Lamplugh Parochial School. He was an accomplished musician and was also the organist at St Michael's for almost

THE CHALLENGE SHIELD.

WON BY
LAMPLUGH CHURCH CHOIR
IN THE YEARS 1912 &1914 AT
WORKINGTON FESTIVAL.

Conductor, Mr C. HALES.

all of the years he taught and lived in the parish. Albert Bethwaite was his successor and played during the 1940s until his sudden death in 1954. William Batey, of Cockan, organist at the Mission Church then took over both churches and continued until he decided to take Holy Orders in the 1960s. (After ordination he held livings in Murton near Appleby, and Moresby). Eleanor Rutherford succeeded him and has been assisted over the years by Betty Marshall, Joyce Litt and Audrey Hedley. Eleanor presently plays for all services at Lamplugh and Kirkland and has been the main organist for over thirty years.

THE OAK PANELLING

The oak panelling round the nave was given in memory of three brave sons of Lamplugh, namely three sons of the Dickinson family of Red How, Capt. Ronald Fryer Bickersteth Dickinson killed in action near Hooge, France, June 1915, Capt. Alan Peile Dickinson killed in action at Le Plantin, France, June 1918, and Capt. George Fryer Dickinson who died, aged 46, in 1932, as a result of wounds and ill health contracted in war. All three were members of the Liverpool Scottish Regiment.

Ronald Fryer Bickersteth Dickinson was born in 1884, educated at Rugby School and qualified as a solicitor in 1910. He was in the first contingent that went over to France in November 1914 and was killed on the same day as his brother George was wounded. George and Alan were also educated at Rugby. Alan, born in 1891, became a Company Commander in June 1915. He arrived in France in February 1917. A shell fatally wounded him in June 1917 during a raid which he led. It was later referred to as 'Dicky's Dash'. He was awarded an M.C. and is buried in Houchin British Cemetery, Pas de Calais.

Other members of the Dickinson family named on the section of brass memorials are Hilary Dickinson and Tamlyn Dickinson, both of whom died in childhood.

LAMPLUGH AND KELTON MEASURES

At one time during the church history, Daniel Dickinson of Streetgate noted (26) that there were two differing land measures for a perch in the Parish of Lamplugh, both of which were marked out on the church wall. They were,

> "1682 December 15. Land measure used within the parish of Lamplugh according to custom and is hereafter mentioned (viz the 'The pearch in Lamplugh is in length 6 yards 1 foot and 9 inches and one quarter of an inch')" and in Kelton, the adjoining township, "it is 6 yards 2 feet 8 inches and three quarter of an inch."

For the measures to be marked on the church wall suggests they were of great importance to the community. They must have fallen into disuse over time, and had outgrown their usefulness. Why were there different measures in the two townships? Was it before joining of the townships? Had it anything to do with tithes? In ancient times markets were sometimes held in the churchyard. Were these measures were used to see that buying and selling met fair play? Acts of 1551 and 1553 made it an excommunication offence to brawl or quarrel in a churchyard. The Lord of the manor in his court could have used them for disputes. There must have been a reason, but at the present time it remains a mystery.

Threshed corn was always sold in bushels and a bushel measure was also kept inside the Church. Did this measure differ in the townships? This remains unanswered too.

THE GARGOYLES

The word gargoyle, like gargle, comes from the Old French word for throat, for the throat of a gargoyle is a spout that drains off the rainwater and throws it clear of the walls. They were made in the image of demons to frighten away any evil spirits or demons that otherwise might have destroyed the church.

There are three gargoyles on the outside of the east wall of the church. These were three of the original spout ends of the previous church, which had no downspouts.

They were placed in this unusual position at the time of the rebuilding. The reason for this might have been to preserve them as a reminder of the old church, to show the beauty and standard of the carving or perhaps the superstition persisted that the gargoyles would still ward off unwanted demons or devils. They might even have been caricatures of some evil spirits or perhaps they were to wish the church and people good luck. It may be that they had some now unknown special significance on the old church. Whatever the reason it is worth looking closely at these carvings using binoculars or a good camera lens, as each one is different and is carved with beautiful patterns. It is recorded that the pre 1870 church was well noted for the high quality of the stone carvings with which it was adorned.

THE LYCH GATES

Many churchyards at the present time are entered via a lych gate. The Old English word 'lich' means corpse and thus 'corpse-gate' (lych gate). It could mean any opening or style by which a cortege could gain access to the churchyard.

A requirement of the 1549 Prayer Book was that the priest should meet the corpse at the church style (gate) and from there should begin the Order for the Burial of the Dead. Later in 1662, the Prayer Book defined that this could be any entrance to the churchyard. Before the 18th century, it was usually the shrouded corpse that was set down

on the corpse table or coffin stools in the lych gate. The affluent members of a village or a town were the only ones to use coffins. As the roads and conditions improved, many parishes gradually acquired a bier for transferring the coffin to the graveside. This was usually a simple wooden frame with four handles. Many old lych gates have bench seats of stone or slate, for the bearers to rest. The bench at Lamplugh is made of wood.

The main entrance to the churchyard before 1870 was more or less opposite Lamplugh Hall stackyard. The present lych gates were given by the Dickinson family of Red How and were built and inscribed by local village tradesmen. The simple but appropriate inscription on the roadside of the gates reads

" The House and Garden of God"
and on the inner side it reads
"Call upon me in the time of trouble
& I will be with thee".

At the time of their installation it was necessary to create a new pathway through the churchyard. Whilst this was being created, numerous old graves and stones had to be removed. Many bones were found in this particular area of the graveyard, all in unnamed graves. It was said, at the time that some of these burials had been past servants from Lamplugh Hall. The remains were collected and 'bagged' together and re-interred near the lych gate. Another source, which was 'word of mouth', said that the bones were interred under the stone slabs of the floor of the gates.

References

24.   Stavridi, M.   Master of Glass – Charles Eamer Kempe 1837 – 1907
25.   Dickinson   P.M. Dickinson, Red How, paper clipping. Date not known
26.   Dickinson, D.   P.M.Dickinson, Red How, Family papers

CHAPTER 7

THE LIVING

In medieval times, the priest was appointed by the lord of the manor and was given a house. He was obliged to carry money for alms with him, to maintain the church, and to provide hospitality to travellers. The priest was usually a commoner by birth. Serfs however, were tied to the land and not allowed to become priests. The priest's duties were to officiate at church services, weddings, baptisms, funerals and to visit the sick. He earned his living from the income from parish lands, fees for services and tithe money. The living at Lamplugh was a Rectory, the patronage of which was always annexed to the Manor and the Rector received his living solely through tithes that were levied upon the parishioners.

In 1291 the living was valued at £23/6/8d (today £23.35p), in 1329 it was £3/6/8d, (today £3.35p) and by 1520 it had crept up to £10/4/6d (today £10.23p). The Border Wars between England and Scotland greatly affected the prosperity and security of Lamplugh, the values fluctuating according to the frequency and severity of the raiding attacks by the Reivers until 1603. In 1768 the living was worth £200 and in 1835, £256. In 1768 the living was bought solely as a commercial transaction. The Rev Richard Dickinson was inducted on 6th May 1768, and

> "did duty at the Parish Church on the Sunday when after which, he advertised the tithes to be let by public auction on the following Friday."(27)

The tithes were commuted in 1839 for a rent charge of £300 a year. Yet the net value of the living in 1901 was only £182. *In 1926 the value was £404 and the patrons were Trustees. By 1938 the net yearly value had risen to "£400, with three acres of glebe and residence" and it was in the patronage of five Trustees. The Rev R. Haythornthwaite B.A., Jesus College, Cambridge held the living in 1938 and had done so since 1909.

*AUGMENTATION OF BENEFICE 1922

> "A meeting was held in the Parochial School to consider the question of raising funds to increase the annual value of the living of Lamplugh. Mr. George Dickinson presided. The present value was £237, which he considered absurdly inadequate for a married clergy with a family who had to keep up the Rectory buildings in addition to all the other numerous calls, which he had to meet. The stipend was equivalent to about 30/- per week pre war. (World War I)." (28)

"In the event of the living becoming vacant the church would be unable to get a man to take it at the present stipend."

"They disliked the idea of either a non-resident priest or of being an annex of a neighbouring parish or to be without a clergyman at all. The alternative being to make a great united effort to raise such a sum as to bring the stipend up to a standard at which a man could live in 'decency and comfort.' " (28)

This had been done in various parishes in the locality. A first response had already raised £200 from the property owners of the Parish and some non-residents. It was finally decided to hold a bazaar in the Lamplugh Council School (now the present school) in May or June (1922).

"The ladies and gentlemen present at the meeting were to constitute the Committee with power to add. Mr. G Dickinson, chairman, Mr. Brooker, Lamplugh Hall, Vice-chairman, Mr. Hy. Wood, treasurer and Messrs. T Boadle and C Hales joint secretaries."(28)

This bazaar appears to have alleviated the problem.

Problems recurred in the late fifties, but it wasn't until 1960 that the benefice became known as 'The Parish of Lamplugh with Ennerdale." From 1960 - 1995 the parish was known by this name. The most recent change to the benefice took place in the Kirkland Mission on Sunday 11th June, 1995 at 3pm. This was the inaugural service to form the new local Ecumenical project for the Church of England Parish of Lamplugh with Ennerdale and the local Methodist Church of Kirkland. So now the present Parish which includes St Michael's Church is officially called "The Ecumenical Parish (Church of England and Methodist Church) of Lamplugh, Kirkland and Ennerdale."

The list of Rectors shows that this was not the first time in St Michael's history the Rector had 'shared' the living with another parish. (1596, 1729, 1772). The reasons in the past could have been because of the huge changes in our social history, e.g. the lack of incumbents and the money needed to provide a reasonable income for the priest and to maintain the buildings.

In 2002 rectors were paid a stipend. Each parish is expected to contribute towards this by paying a yearly sum, namely a quota, to help finance the clergy, the cost of their pensions and housing. The quota for 1994 was £13,677, an increase of £1,700 on the previous year. The churches in the dioceses are all asked to help meet the increasing share of the cost of this 'stipend package' An independent report in 1994 confirmed that the Church commissioners could not afford to continue their support of clergy pay and pensions. It is a well-known fact that unwise investments in the late 1980s by the Church of England had contributed towards this state of affairs. New arrangements to share these costs were discussed. In April 1995 an agreement was reached, and dioceses would be asked to meet the cost (from funds provided by parishes) of all pension rights which will be earned by clergy from future service. To help raise the quota, some parishioners and supporters covenant a regular sum of money each year. Fetes, Auctions, Flower Festivals and other fund raising efforts supplement this income.

BUILDING OF KIRKLAND MISSION

The reason for the building of the Kirkland Mission was because of the huge rise in the population in the Kirkland area of the parish due to the mining and quarrying boom after 1860. The Lamplugh Parochial Church Council funded the building. Consequently numerous large and small fund raising activities took place. On one occasion the then Countess of Lowther (Lord Lonsdale was Lord of Kelton, Kirkland is within this township.) and Mrs. Brooksbank 'a Lamplugh' descendant, along with the parishioners of St Michael's held a huge bazaar in Whitehaven. A new porch was added to the mission in 1993, as was an improved entrance path. Permission for an extension to the Mission in 1994 was requested and grants were applied for from various bodies. It was duly built and came into use during 1995. The name given to the new extension was agreed to be 'The Chapel Room'.

Church Council and Sidesmen in front of the Lamplugh Rectory taken between 1880 - 1888
Back row: Mr Graham Kirkland, ?, ?, Joe Kneen, Fell Dyke, Matthew Jackson, ?, Bowness,
Whinnah, ?, ? Frears, Kirkland. Middle row: Harry Mossop, ?, ?, Joseph Dickinson, Red How, Rev James
Macarthur, ?, ?, ?, John Brown High House Front Row: ?, ?, John Sloan, Isaac Holmes, Bill Sewell

THE PAROCHIAL CHURCH COUNCIL

'The whole system of Parochial Church Council, Deanery, Diocesan and General Synod elections is based on Parishes' Electoral Rolls. These rolls are the first stage in the representation of lay people in the decision making of the Church of England. Membership of the church Electoral Roll gives the right to attend and vote at Annual Church meetings where elections take place for Parochial Church Councils and Parishes' representatives on the Deanery Synod. In turn Deanery Synod members, elect representatives on to Diocesan Synods and the General Synod. The Electoral Rolls are constantly revised but every six years they are prepared again from scratch. No names may be carried forward from the old roll to the newly prepared roll; everyone who wishes to remain on the roll must re-apply. These rules apply to every Parish. (29)

A newspaper report of a Lamplugh Parochial Church Council meeting dated 1934

"Touching reference to the splendid work of the late George Dickinson and the late Mr. A. Harris was made at the annual meeting of St Michael's Lamplugh, on Monday, Rev R. Haythornthwaite presiding. Mr. Henry Wood was appointed Rector's warden: Messrs. H. Smith, J. Jackson and E. Douglas, people's wardens, and the following the sidesmen; Messrs R. Batey, T. Boadle, J. H. Frears, H. J. Wood, J. Rutherford and J. R. Wilkinson. The church accounts showed a balance of £20 10s 3d: and the Kirkland Mission accounts (presented by Mr. H Smith) a balance of £11 16s 7d. The Ruri-decanal Conference representatives were re-elected as follow: Messrs E. Douglas, C. Hales and H. Wood. Mr. Hales was appointed delegate to the Diocesan Conference in the room of the late Mr. Dickinson. The Chairman moved a comprehensive vote of thanks, Mr. Hales seconding."(30)

In comparison in 1989 the Lamplugh with Ennerdale Parochial Church Council balance sheet showed that the expenditure for that year was £18,900-39 and that the income was £16,706-47, the excess expenditure over income was £2193-92.

CHURCHWARDENS

Churchwardens were first appointed in the 12th century so this important office has survived for more than 800 years. Churchwardens took over from the parishioners the maintenance of the church fabric and had the authority to haul people before ecclesiastical courts, where moral and religious offences were judged.

In the Middle Ages they needed to be good businessmen and after the Reformation they played an active role in local government. If they were elected by the parish but refused the office they could be heavily fined. By the 17th Century, churchwardens, who by then were assisted by sidesman, were overseeing parish taxes alongside the parish clerks. They ensured the Parish Registers were kept by the minister, could arrest unlicensed hawkers and pedlars, receive fines levied on persons for gaming and drunkenness, and had duties regarding the Poor Laws. They had to keep careful accounts of income from church properties and land. In 1775 Humphrey Senhouse of Cross Cannonby,

> "was threatened with proceedings in the Consistory Court by the churchwardens for failing to contribute towards the cost of repairing or making a new east window in the church, and in 1792 , the minister, Joseph Gilbanks, was deprived for notorious drunkenness"(31)

The churchwarden's office changed very little over the 18th and 19th centuries, especially in villages. The biggest and most radical change was in 1921, when parish councils took over all parochial lay financial responsibilities, thus leaving churchwardens as honorary officers assisting the parson.

There is evidence that the churchwardens at St Michael's witnessed that the registers were regularly checked and that they were kept in order, because at the bottom of most pages, especially in the earlier church registers, their signatures appear with 'churchwarden' underneath. The handwriting differs from that of the priest so they were men who were able to read and write. A churchwardens' account book still exists, and can be found at the Whitehaven Record Office. It gives entries of their expenses.

The church wall seems to have caused them concern; during one period it was frequently giving way and crumbling and so had to be constantly repaired. The Lamplugh churchwardens' staffs of office are kept in the nave near the back of the church opposite to the font. They are made of plain wood and are mounted with a cross.

In 2003 the churchwardens were Martha Jackson, Cyril Atkinson and Malcolm Robson.

References

27.	Dickinson, J	Bound Memo of John Dickinson
28.	Dickinson	Local Newspaper clipping, title unknown
29.	Davis, Alan	Grass Roots; Churchwardens' papers
30.	Dickinson	Red How, Newspaper Clipping. 1934,
31.	Hughes, E	North Country Life in 19th century Vol. II Cumberland and Westmorland 1700 – 1830, OUP
32.	Churchwardens	Vestry meetings, Minute and Account books

Lamplugh July 1770 Churchwardens Account Book

"Notice is hereby given that a vestry will be held in this Church on Thursday ye 19th inst. In pursuance of a Mandate received from ye Right Reverend ye Lord Bishop of Chester, to consider about repairing ye church and other special business:

MEMORANDUM

At a Vestry held by proclamation as above in ye parish of Lamplugh on this 19th Day of July one thousand seven hundred and seventy, We ye Churchwardens (etc.) do think ye following repairs necessary: viz

That ye floor of ye sd. Parish Church be laid anew
That ye seats be repair'd and backed after ye modern fashion
That ye church be ceil'd.
That ye pulpit, reading desk be placed in ye middle of ye church.
We the parishioners met at this Vestry do hereunto sign our names assenting to or dissenting from the said repairs

For:	Against:
John Dickinson	Wm. Dale
John Bowman	John Dixon
Jos. Bowman	Peter Pearson
John Jenkinson	
Jon Bowman's, His mark I= =	
Joseph Mason	
John Braithwaite, Churchwarden	
Henry Dixon, Churchwarden // his mark	
Abraham Little	
Anthony Branthwaite	
Joseph Bowman."	

Entries taken from the Churchwardens' Vestry Minute book:

"April 1878, Meeting in the vestry of church at 6.30p.m. Four churchwardens appointed. Mr Brooksbank had given land to extend the churchyard and proposed by Jos. Dickinson that Mr Brooksbank should have a plot of ground resigned to him for a family burial. Mr Dickinson suggested that some record of interesting events should be kept, such as the gift of the land and proposed a minute book be procured."

1879 Nave insured for £1200;

1881 Brass lamps purchased for the Chancel.

1892 Sidesmen to be increased to eight: - J Dickinson, M. Jackson, J. Wilkinson, J. Bowman, J. Yates, M. Thomas, W. Batey, I. Frears.

1896 Accounts had an adverse balance of £3. 10s 0d as well as a debt to the Mission Room Fund. Reasons given - serious frost and gales of winter of 1894/5. Apathetic feeling on part of congregation; the extra effort had not been made.

1901 Discussion on provision of hymn books for strangers.

1903 Mr..... pointed out that the stained glass windows recently added had very much darkened the church thus making it necessary to use more artificial light and causing extra expenditure for oil. He suggested that those responsible for the insertion of these windows should be asked to contribute a sum of money to the church funds sufficient to meet the extra expense thus incurred. The chairman undertook to interview those concerned. The expenditure for oil has nearly been doubled. Accounts show a loss - on occasions the offertory was omitted on account of storm.

1908 Expenditure £37.3s 4d; Receipts £39.13s.2d"(32)

CHAPTER 8
TITHES

A tithe was originally a tax of one tenth of all produce payable to the local clergyman by his land-owning parishioners. Tithes were payable in kind. Payment of tithes was made compulsory in the 10th century and could be enforced by both civil and ecclesiastical authorities. They were 'taxes' to maintain the church and provide help or relief to the poor. Produce raised as tithes was stored in the parish, usually in the tithe barns.

Margaret Allen in her book "Hesket Newmarket" states that it was in about the year 690, Ina, King of the West Saxons made a new law that said,

> "The first fruits of seeds, or church due, arising from the product of corn etc. are to be paid at the feast of St. Martin; and let him that fails in payment forfeit 40s."

In 1784 the tithes in Lamplugh were let by public auction for £96 (being worth £102). This bid was some £16 better than that obtained previously. The Glebe Land (the piece of land serving as part of the clergyman's benefice and providing income) was let for £6 per year.

The Tithe Commutation Act of 1836/7 provided the framework for tithes to be changed to rent-charges or cash payments. Detailed maps had to be drawn up and commissioners were appointed to negotiate land values in the parishes. The maps indicated the boundaries of individual fields and the existence of buildings such as barns and stables as well as dwellings. Each property was identified by a number, which was shown on the tithe map. Areas were measured in acres, roods and poles, there being 4 roods in one acre and 40 poles in one rood. The map also indicated whether a field was arable, pasture or woodland. Copies of the survey records can be found at the Public Record Office in Whitehaven.

These awards recorded that the whole quantity of land subject to Tithes within the parish of Lamplugh (i.e. cultivated as arable and subject to tithes) was estimated at 1,509 acres. The owner of Low Leys in 1837 was the Rev. George Lewthwaite, the occupier was Thomas Boyd. He held 91 acres 1 rood 10 poles and paid a tithe of £8 7s 1d. Thomas Boyd also occupied Middle Leys, which was 47 acres 2 roods 9 poles and paid a tithe of £4 16s 11d. Lancelot Coulthard of Cockan who held 47 acres 3 roods 39 poles paid a tithe of £4 4s 2d. The tithe map of 1837 shows that a field next to number 334 on Cockan Farm was owned by Trinity Chapel, Whitehaven. The field on the opposite side and adjoining the field is Priest How, the field in which Kirkland Mission stands. The history of church connections in this area of Kelton still requires further research.

An Act in 1891 restricted the payment of tithes to land owners and the Tithe Act of 1925 transferred tithe rent charges to the Queen Anne's Bounty Fund (established in 1704) to receive and administer funds for the benefit of the poorer clergy. Tithes were ended by the Tithe Act of 1936. Some glebe rent was still being paid in Lamplugh in the 1940s.

Most parishes once possessed a tithe barn but few have survived. The ruins of what was at one time the tithe barn of Lamplugh can just be seen on the right hand side of the road almost at the top of Cockan Brow, between the School Corner (near Dhustone & the Women's Institute) to Kirkland. The tithe barn had been converted into two cottages at some time after it was no longer used for its original purpose. Census records of 1881 give the names of the families living there. Two families were still living there in the 1940s. The two dwellings, which were named Pansy Cottages, are now ruins and only foundation rubble is left. The rectangular heap does however give some idea of its size.

TITHING CUSTOMS IN LAMPLUGH

Some of the tithing customs of Lamplugh recorded in 1771 by Richard Dickinson, Rector of Lamplugh and were as follows:

"Corn is pay'd in kind through the whole parish and the manner of takeinge is this. The Owner cuts down, binds up and stooks the Corn, and the Parson by the Owners consent sets out every tenth Stook and tenth part with liberty to dry his Corn on the stubel."

"To the said Rectory is also belonging the tithe of Wool. And the Ancient custom concerning it is this: the Owner lays it in five heapes and the Rector takes one and divides that in two and the Owner takes one half back again, but no Hogg wool is pay'd."

Tithe of Geese is pay'd at Michaelmas, two out of every flock.

Every person keeping Bees pays for every swarm a Penny.

Every Hous pays 4d for a hen, but no eggs, and it is pay'd at Easter.

Every wedding by bands one shilling, by licence five shillings.

For a funeral, sixpence without a sermon.

Tithe of piggs is one out of every litter.

For every Communicant after the first time of Receiving is three Halfpence pay'd on Easter Tuesday.

Every person who has ten calves pays four shillings for Five and any number under Ten only Two shillings. For every new Milk Cow twopence. For every Hand or Stript Milk Cow only a half penny. Calves and Milk is pay'd on Easter Tuesday at the Parsonage House.

Every Tenyment pays Threepence prescription yearly at Easter in lieu of Hay and Roots.

A Fole a penny.

Kelton Mill pays two shillings and sixpence to the Rector on Easter Tuesday.

Mortuary according to Act of Parliament.

There is a custom in the parish if any person break fresh ground never before plow'd if he make an improvement o it and do not worsen his other Tithe and shows no defraud by it he has it tithe free for Seven years first after such improvement.

The Parson has right of common on all the Commons in the Parish." (33)

Information concerning revenue from tithes, dues, offerings, clerical incomes, the size of parsonage houses and local concerns can be found in glebe Terriers. They were first required in 1571 and were reviewed and updated periodically in each diocese thereafter.

The parson employed tithe leaders to gather up his wool and corn in Lamplugh because he was entitled to the 'Great Tithe.' They then carted it up to the tithe barn. A 'Great Tithe' was awarded to a parson who was sole incumbent. He received all the customary offerings and dues of the parish with the proviso that he was responsible for the chancel, rectory, providing service books and vestments. In parishes where the rector was not the incumbent, the tithes were apportioned between the rector (which might be a collegiate or a monastic foundation) and a vicar, who was appointed to deputise but take charge of a parish. This was known as a Small or Vicarial Tithe. The money collected was known as 'Easter Dues' and was collected at the Parsonage during every Easter week. The old customs of collection in kind and payments were made according to the numbers of stock. The actual sum payable or value of the tithe rent charge still varied from year to year according to the price of wheat, barley and oats. An annual list was published to assist the parson and the owner to calculate a figure from the rent charge apportionment.

Mr R. F. Dickinson notes that the apportionments in the parish of Lamplugh contain numerous pencil annotations made by the Rev R. Haythornthwaite, the Rector to whom, as late as the 1930s, the keeping up to date of the list was of great personal and practical concern. In the late 1950s it was customary to give all monies collected at the Easter Sunday Services in Lamplugh and Kirkland to the Rector.

References
33.   Dickinson, R.F.   'Tithing customs of West Cumberland,' C&WAAS 1960 Vol. LX New Series.

Lamplugh Church Terrier for 1810

*Copied from the registry at Chester

It...One mansion or dwelling house

It...One barn near the Parsonage House with a stable and one Bire joined to the South East end of the same.

It...One garden of about half a rood of ground but no orchard.

It...Another barn a mile distant from the parsonage House and more.

It... Glebe and about two acre lying on the backside of the Parsonage House. No meadow or pasture land belonging to the Rectory.

It...One tenement belonging to the Rectory called by the name of Kirkland, which pays eight shillings yearly rent to the Rector of Lamplugh, four shillings at Easter and four shillings at Michaelmas, and we have heard that a fine of eight pounds has been formerly paid to the Rector at the death of a tenant.

(1734 terrier says eight shillings yearly but no fine at all)

It...No lands or Estates are tithe free within the Parish save the Demesne lands of the House of Lamplugh which only pays Prescription ten shillings per annum in lieu of all manner of tithes.

It... The rest of the Parish pays all the tithe corn in kind. Lamb and wool are in kind. Hay is not paid in kind and prescription some more, some less.

It... Ten shillings for a mortuary if it be forty pounds and upwards if the Inventory be so much debtless. If under twenty pounds three shillings four pence.

OBLATION

It... Every communicant after the time of receiving the sacrament one penny halfpenny but at the first time of receiving only a halfpenny.

It... For every new milch cow two pence. Every stript cow a halfpenny.

It...Every tithe calf four shillings half a tithe calf two shillings

It...Mine rent, belonging to Stockhow two shillings yearly. The Minister hath the Right of Commons and Beasts Pasture.

(1734 says: - No pasture for Beasts but right of Common to the Rectory.)

It... Tithe hens and geese and pigs etc

Geo Lamplugh, Rector of Lamplugh

William Fleming, X his mark, Henry Wood, Lancelot Dixon, William Fox, Churchwardens.

This is a true copy examined with the Terrier remaining in the Registry of Chester

Endorsed: - Richard Dickinson Rector of Lamplugh Sept. 19th 1810

From the papers belonging to the late R. F. Dickinson, loaned by Mrs P.M. Dickinson.

CHAPTER 9
THE CHURCH REGISTERS 1581 – 1812

Thomas Cromwell, Lord Privy Seal to Henry VIII, introduced a mandate in September 1538 that said

> " That every person, vicar or curate should enter in a book every wedding, christening and burial in his parish. The entries had to be made each Sunday in the presence of one of the Wardens. They were usually made on paper, sometimes on loose sheets and so the survival rate of these earliest registers is poor" (34)

Elizabeth I directed that the records from 1538 had to be continued to be written into books from the beginning of her reign (1558). So many parish registers begin circa 1558. All registers had to be kept in a protective box, later known as the 'Parish Chest'. The chests were usually made with planks of oak. Some were large, others small, some just a tree trunk roughly hewn out in the middle and some were beautifully carved. Sometimes later, because of their age, they had to have iron bands placed around them to keep them together. The chests had to have three locks with a key. One key was held by the Parson, and one each by the churchwardens. There must at one time have been such a chest standing in Lamplugh Church. Perhaps it might have stood there until 1870.

A chest does stand in the vestry but it is not a parish chest. Within living memory a small metal safe was used at St Michael's for the keeping of documents etc. This safe was used until a larger and more secure one was purchased. This latter safe, dated 1855, was the one that was originally purchased and used by the Lamplugh Friendly Society. The last Treasurer and Secretary, Tom Blacklock, on behalf of the Society, sold it when the Club ceased to the postmistress of Lamplugh, Mary Ann Hannah. She used it in the post office (now The Old Post Office) until she retired in the 1960s. It was then sold to John Stalker, who purchased it for the use of the church. It appears not to have been secure enough for today's world, as recently (2002), someone managed to damage the mechanism in an attempt to steal its contents. It held only the obligatory church papers.

It was not until 1732 that the Parish registers were ordered to be written in English. Fortunately the Lamplugh Registers are in English throughout and not Latin, unlike a large number of pre-1732 registers. Sometimes there can be confusion about year dates that are given in the registers and this is due to the change that was made from the Julian Calendar to the Gregorian Calendar in 1751/1752, (Lord Chesterfield's Act) The Julian Calendar ran from 25th March to the 24th March. The Gregorian Calendar runs from 1st January to the 31st December, beginning on 1st January,

1752 but excluded 11 days from and including, 3rd to the 13th September of that year. In 1812 - 1813 parish registers had to be laid out in a formal fashion and with group entries, Baptisms, Marriages and Burials had their own register. (The Rose or Parochial Registers Act.) This remains so today. Civil registration of births, marriages and deaths began in England and Wales on 1st July 1837.

We are fortunate that the Lamplugh Registers dated as above, except for the years 1661- 1684, still exist. There is written evidence that there were some records before 1581, but as they were not kept in a bound book, but on loose papers, they must have gradually deteriorated, torn or showed signs of decay, and so eventually become either lost or not thought to be worthwhile keeping. The various transcriptions of the registers, which now exist, are based on the work of the Parish Register section of the Cumberland and Westmorland Antiquarian and Archaeological Society (C&WAAS).

The three earliest registers

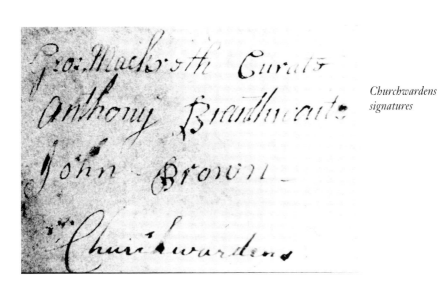

Churchwardens signatures

"THE PREFACE TO REGISTERS OF LAMPLUGH "

The following is a copy of the description, regarding the condition of the registers, written for the Parish Register Section of the Cumberland and Westmorland Antiquarian Society. The transcription is by Col. Francis Haswell, C.I.E., M.D., of Penrith, and the indexing by Charles S. Jackson, Esq. of Yanwath. (35)

"1581 - 1812

These registers from the commencement in 1581 to 1812 consist of five volumes. They are all of parchment, except the printed marriage forms of volume five.

Volume I. (1581 - 1660.)

This has had a hard life, the first four pages having been destroyed and mice having eaten into the next twenty-four, thus destroying some of the entries; the first existing page has been scribbled over and is practically undecipherable. The sequence of years is not regular, but this is certainly because at some later period the volume has been rebound. The entries were originally well arranged by the separation of the Baptisms, Marriages and Burials, for each year. It will be noticed that until the year 1595, when a new Rector succeeded Tristram Warwick, the years commenced in the modern form and subsequently Lancelot Fletcher began in the usual way on March 25th. The text is English throughout.

Volume II (1684 - 1724.)

This is a small book of twenty-two pages, which has suffered from dampness; it is unfortunately in a very small handwriting for the first half and partially illegible; the Burials on the first four pages are in an unusual form. The commencement shows that a gap of 24 years occurs at this interesting time in history.

Volume III (1725 - 1769.)

This is in good condition and well written; the marriages here cease in 1753.

Volume IV (1769 - 1812.)

This consists of Baptisms and Burials only; it is well arranged and written by the Curates of the time, except the last three pages, which deteriorate.

Volume V (1753 - 1812.)

Contains Marriages only in printed forms, many in duplicate, because the originals were suffering from damp.
There are numerous entries of the well-known families of Lamplugh* - Rawling, Dickinson, also one or two of Lowther and Kirkby.
Signed by F. H. (Francis Haswell)."

(*To these could be added Bowman, Branthwaite, Dixon, Jackson, Patrickson, Robinson, Rodgers, Skelton and Wood. (B.M.))

References

34.   Parish Registers website – 'parish registers'   Registers of Lamplugh, 1581 – 1812, C&WAAS,
35.   Haswell, Col. F. H. & Jackson C. S.   Parish Register Section 1936.

CHAPTER 10
REGISTER ENTRIES AND RELATED TRADITIONS

BAPTISM

Since the 3rd century, children born of Christian parents have been baptised in infancy. An exception did occur during the 4th century when baptism was deferred until death was imminent. In ecclesiastical law, a layman can legally baptise in an emergency. In the Middle Ages midwives were licensed by bishops and were told that under no circumstances should they neglect baptism in the presence of witnesses if there was any likelihood of the child dying before the arrival of a priest. The mother would not be present as no woman was allowed to enter church after she had given birth until she had been 'churched', a service of thanksgiving for the birth. Since the Reformation, baptism has followed the Book of Common Prayer and since 1980 the Alternative Service Book. It was not until June 1786 that the law required that a mother's maiden name had to be included in the baptismal records.

It was not unusual for those who could not afford a doctor to attend a birth, to ask a recognised local woman to help to deliver the baby. Sometimes doctors when called in to attend a birth would send for local women to help them. These women learned through experience and became quite skilled at their task without any formal training. They were sometimes known as 'Parish mothers.' It was at one time usual for the friends of middle-class women to be 'bidden' to attend births. A large dish of rum butter was usually made in readiness for 'the Day' and the new mother was the first recipient. Sometimes the baby's head was washed with rum to 'strengthen it.' Part of this Cumberland tradition still exists but now the rum butter is provided with cream crackers at the Christening. There are many Cumbrian houses that still have a special family bowl, often an heirloom, which is solely used for this purpose. Rum butter is made with rum, butter, and soft brown sugar with sometimes a sprinkling of cinnamon or nutmeg. Today the recipe varies slightly and rum butter is sold commercially in large quantities to tourists.

The first legible entry in the Church Baptismal register is in 1581 and dated April 18th.

Richard Fox son of .... ; The second is ...Richard Patrickson........ of Stackay.

MARRIAGES

THE ORIGIN AND HISTORY OF SOME MARRIAGE CUSTOMS

It is said that the earliest marriages were by capture where the groom, helped by his warrior friends, his best men, kidnapped a woman from another tribe's camp. His friends covered his back, fighting off others who had an interest in the woman whilst he held her with his left hand leaving his right hand free, as his sword hand, to defend himself and his bride. This is believed to be the root of the custom of the bride standing on the groom's left during the wedding ceremony. This custom was carried out through many centuries until eventually it evolved into becoming a marriage by purchase.

The word 'wedding' comes from the Anglo-Saxon word 'wedd' meaning to wager or gamble. It referred to the vow the man gave to marry another man's daughter or to the goods or bride price. Women were bought for breeding purposes by the grooms and sold for land, status, political alliances or occasionally cash. The modern practice of the bride and groom exchanging gifts and the question of whose family pays for what is rooted in the ancient customs of bride price and dowry.

After families agreed on the price, goods were exchanged at the 'handfasting', with local priests among the witnesses. Giving the bride away derives from the 'marriage by purchase,' when the father handed his daughter over to her master. Today it is connected with the love between the father and his daughter. The father hands over the responsibility of caring for his daughter to the man she has chosen to marry.

Upper class Romans were married by priests, but not the common people. After Britain was converted to Christianity, one of the first things the church took on was the wedding. Couples only went to church to have the union blessed until eventually the church took over the whole event from witnesses, moving on to blessing the ring and the joining of hands. They then turned what was a business arrangement into a full religious affair. Later the Archbishop of Canterbury ordered that all weddings be publicly announced for three Lord's Days, and that marriages should be celebrated in the Church with reverence in daylight in the face of the congregation. Priests used the threat of excommunication to prevent secret engagements and weddings. Until the reign of Edward VI the ceremony was performed at the door of the church with everybody then moving inside for Mass.

The wearing of a white dress did not become popular until the Victorian era. For centuries there were no wedding dresses. A wealthy bride wore fancier versions of her everyday clothes, others wore their best dress, often decorated with ribbon and garlands. The first mention of a white wedding dress being worn was by Ann of Brittany in 1499. There are no more until 1530 when the daughter of Henry VII, Margaret Tudor, married James IV of Scotland. Mary Queen of Scots defied tradition and wore white when she married the Dauphin of France (white was at that time the mourning colour for French Queens). In Elizabethan times white became a symbol of pure young maidenhood and an automatic colour for brides. However it was Queen Victoria who popularised the white wedding custom that we know today.

The bridesmaid is another tradition we owe to the Anglo-Saxons. Before Christianity, in the time of the Druids, it was believed that evil spirits jealous of the happiness of the couple, would create mischief for them. To confuse the spirits the bride's and groom's friends dressed identically to them to ensure that the jealous ones could not pick them out. This belief faded with Christianity but the custom did not.

The modern bouquet has its origins in antiquity. Egyptian, Ancient Greek and Roman brides, carried sheaves of wheat, a strong symbol of fertility. They wore flowers on their heads.

The tradition of wearing a wedding ring on the third finger of the left hand stems from the Ancient Greeks, some say the Egyptians. Their belief was that a nerve ran directly from that finger to the heart, giving the groom the illusion that he had placed a ring round the bride's heart. Another explanation is that the ring worn on the left hand was to signify the subjugation of the bride to her husband. The right hand signifies power, independence and authority. Another is that the third finger can't be straightened unless the other fingers are extended, which makes it safer there. Left-handed people were considered to be sinister (the latin for left-handed is 'senester') and to belong to the devil so every one avoided predominantly using that hand.

There has always been a cake. The Egyptians, Greeks and Romans crumbled thin grain cakes over the head of the bride to symbolise her fertility. In the Middle Ages, it became popular to have the bride and groom try to kiss over a tower of smaller cakes. A success meant prosperity for the couple, but it was during the reign of Charles II that the cake as we know today became popular. In the 1700s it became a tradition to thread a small piece of the cake through the wedding ring a certain number of times and sleep with it beneath the pillow. Before going to sleep a prayer was said. Over time it became popular to box up small pieces of cake for the maids and bachelors to take home.

In Anglo-Saxon times when the father of the bride gave his daughter to the groom he also gave him her shoe to show whose property she was and to transfer his authority. The groom then immediately hit the bride on the head with the shoe to show her who was master in their relationship. It was then taken to the bridal chamber and placed over the husband's side of the bed. In time it became the custom to throw shoes at the bridal couple, a practice which continued through until Victorian times. With the invention of motor cars it became more practical for the guests to tie shoes to the departing car. In this way, the shoes still followed behind the couple. The old rhyme,

> "Something old. Something new. Something borrowed.
> Something blue, a silver sixpence for the shoe"

appeared in Victorian times.

The ancient fertility custom of throwing grain over the departing couple has never gone away. When rice became cheaper than other grains, it was substituted. Today the fertility meaning is lost, but the ritual goes on with the use of either rice or confetti.

BIDDEN WEDDINGS

In close knit societies such as existed in past Lakeland Cumberland a 'Bidden Wedding' was an opportunity for the entire district to socialise and have a 'reet good time.' An open invitation to the wedding was made by the use of local posters or by notices in the local newspaper 'bidding' people to attend. Music by a fiddler, dancing and noisy revelry with prizes for competitions were the order of the day. To be invited to a 'bidden wedding' was regarded as a mark of respect, especially by women. (36)

The bridegroom would get up early in the morning and with his closest friends go on horseback to have breakfast with his bride. The couple often followed a fiddler to the church. This custom still occurs in Norway. After the ceremony the wedding party would then proceed to the local alehouse to drink the health of the newly wed couple. Then a race at full speed on foot or on horseback, back to the bride's home, took place. A handkerchief was presented to the first person to reach the bride's house. A huge meal followed with songs from local singers, dancing to the fiddler's tunes, wrestling and other sports would take place. (See poem quoted on page 87) These activities were an accepted part of the celebrations.

The custom of breaking the wedding cake over the bride's head by the husband followed. This was a thin currant cake not like the elaborate iced cakes of today. The bride's head was covered with a white cloth and the bridegroom stood behind her, then the broken pieces were given to the 'guests'. Later the bride sat in state while the guests placed money and other gifts in a plate on her knee.

Another custom was called the 'bridewain'. This took place at the bridegroom's house. When the bride and her furniture were taken to the new home in a 'wain' or a wagon. The population for many miles around was invited to attend. They would find a dish on the table. Guests contributed according to their means. The sum collected could be large and the success of the wedding was judged by the amount collected. Some Lake Poets refer to the 'wain' in which the bride sent all her belongings to her new home. It would consist of an oak chest containing bed linen, hand-woven rugs, blankets, a spinning wheel and bits and pieces of furniture as well as the gifts of her friends. About 1750, the 'bridewain' came to mean to being the collection of money taken by newly-weds at their wedding breakfast. This custom has changed again, so that today the couples who are to marry, now have lists of presents that can be given to the guests as this contains specific items the couple would like to receive.

In his book " The History of Arlecdon and Frizington" the Rev E. H. Sugden writes about a "Bidden Wedding". He records an actual advertisement taken from the 'Paquet' Newspaper.

Report of a Bidden Wedding – Taken from the 'Paquet' June 1785.

"Suspend for one day all your care and your labours,
And come to this wedding, kind friends and good neighbours."

"Notice is hereby given, that the marriage of Isaac Pearson with Frances Atkinson will be solemnized in due form in the Parish Church of Lamplugh, on Monday next, the 30th May, instant, immediately after which the bride and bridegroom, with attendants, will proceed to Lonefoot (Lanefoot) in the said Parish, where the nuptials will be celebrated by the variety of rural entertainments.

"Then come one and all,
At Hymen's soft call,
From Whitehaven, Workington, Harrington, Dean,
Haile, Ponsonby, Blaing, and all places between;
From Egremont, Cockermouth, Parton, Saint Bees,
Dint, Kinneyside, Calder, and parts joining these,
Such sports there will be as have seldom been seen,
Such wrestling and fencing and dancing between;
And races for prizes and frolic and fun,
By horses, by asses, and dogs will be run,
And you'll all go home happy as sure as a gun.
In a word such a wedding can ne'er fail to please,
For the sports of Olympus were trifles to these.
Nota Bene, you'll please to observe that the day
Of this grand bridal pomp is the thirtieth of May,
When 'tis hop'd that the sun to enliven the sight,
Like the Flambeau of Hymen, will deign to burn bright.
Lamplugh, May 20th, 1786"

A tradition that occurs at Lamplugh and Lakeland weddings, though not so frequent in latter years, is when the guests and bridal party went into church, the children who were onlookers remained outside and tied up the church gates. After the ceremony the wedding party were not allowed to leave or to be free to untie the ropes until they threw or scattered money outside the gates for the children to collect. When cars arrived on the scene it became customary to hold a rope tautly across the road to stop the cars moving forward. Money was thrown from the bridal cars for the children to catch or pick up from the ground and not until then were the cars allowed to pass. Many local people in the parish and Cumbria will have memories of taking part in one or other of these events. In the 1940s and 1950s children called them ' a shill out' or 'a scrammel,' supposedly because the children scrambled around on the ground collecting the money that had been 'shilled' or thrown out. Tying the gate was known as 'the snecking' up of the gate.

What the origins of this tradition are is lost but according to Walter McIntyre in 'Lakeland and the Borders of Long Ago,' it might have been a relic of old tribal life, when it was considered necessary for a maiden to marry a man not of her own tribe. This was when she had to be bought or taken by force and the tying up is a survival of a show of force.

Rev Sugden states that in 1897 the children demanded 'ball money' from the wedding party. The men paid 3d (now 1½ new pence) each; if booted and spurred they paid 6d. (3p) Women gave nothing. He also recorded that the money in some parishes was spent on coal for the school fire, but in Arlecdon it was chiefly spent on sweets. G. Findler in his book on Folklore refers to this tradition as 'the demanding of passage money from the bridegroom.' He also records that 'the workmates of the happy pair would stretch a rope cross the road or near the entrance of the church, and would not allow the newly weds to pass until a shower of coins had been thrown and scrambled for.' The bridegroom had to pay for safe conduct so that he and his bride could proceed safely on their new life together.

There is a very humorous dialect account called **"T' story ov a bidden weddin' in Lampla"** written by John Sewell in the 1954 edition of the Journal of the Lakeland Dialect Society. He describes a 'shellout' as follows

> "Ameast ivverboddy in t'village war invitet, an yan o' t' biggest an' best ivver Bidden Weddin, that com off at Lonnin' Feut, Lampla was when Tom Braythet was weddit ta Fanny Leethet. As seune as t'weddin party cum oot o't' kirk theer was sec a frappin o'guns an' pistols as nivver was hard (heard) afore. ' T' shutters (those who tied the gates) gat a laal matter o'brass an' meade off for Lampla Cross (local pub) ta sup t'brass they'd gitten. Doon at Fitz Brig two chaps frae Smaithet hed a heavy car across t'rwoad blocken t'way, and doon at Whinna t'rwoad was blockt wid a pleugh, a par o' Sheloins, an a car- reape (rope) tied abeune them, an annudder shellout hed ta be meade".

In many places it is considered unlucky for the future bridegroom on the day of the wedding to see his bride before the marriage.

THE READING OF BANNS

The reading of the banns was first ordered to take place in England in 1200 in order to prevent people who were too closely related entering into marriage and to provide time for any member of the community to make objections to the match. Before 1754 there were numerous ways of entering marriage. One option was the publication of banns or the obtaining of a special licence followed by a church wedding or being married in the porch. The latter was partly to avoid expense and partly because it was acceptable in the eyes of society. Being married at the door was legal in common law, even though the Church disapproved of it. In St Michael's Church Lamplugh, banns are normally read from the chancel. The reading of banns has to take place in the churches of the parishes in which the bride and the bridegroom are residing.

In the Lamplugh registers there is evidence of the Justices of the Peace having had power to carry out marriages. 'John Nicholson of Boutle aged 30, Mrs. Elizabeth Furnace, aged 26. Married at Lamplugh the 20th of July 1654 by Thos. Lamplugh, Justice of ye Peace.'

> "This is also evidence of the operation of Puritan Rule when marriage ceased to be a religious ceremony and was performed before a magistrate. The Banns were not published in Church but in the Market Place or Local Fair Days"

To date there is no evidence where the banns were published in Lamplugh during the Commonwealth. It can only be presumed that the Local Justices of the Peace, most likely the Lamplugh family, such as Thomas Lamplugh kept the records and they were later deposited or kept at some lawful place. There is documentary evidence showing that one Justice of the Peace in Cumberland kept records during the time of the Commonwealth, 1649-1660:

> "There are many such marriages recorded in a note book of William Thompson of Thornflatts, Justice of the Peace for Cumberland, had kept records during the Commonwealth." (37)

So perhaps further records are yet to be found.

In 1753 Lord Hardwick's Marriage Act said that by law marriages had to be called by banns and a licence obtained. These had also to be recorded separately in the registers, not with baptisms and burials. The Act was designed to prevent clandestine marriages, such as penniless men running off with heiresses. There must have been many such clandestine marriages. Evidence shows many were carried out by unscrupulous priests. After the Act, the register had to show the place of residence of both parties and had to be signed by the groom, bride and two witnesses. It was also necessary to record if the marriage was by licence or following the publication of banns. Marriages had to be performed in the parish church for all except Quakers and Jews. The Catholic Church was not allowed to carry out marriage ceremonies, but many Catholic priests defied the Act. The Act also stated that consent to a marriage had to be given by parents if either party was under 21 years of age. Since the Act did not apply in Scotland, it was the origin of the trend for eloping to Gretna Green, the first or nearest village over the border.

Following the above Act, the Marriage Acts of 1823 and 1836 stated that while marriages without banns or a licence were valid, any minister who officiated at such a marriage was a felon.

DEATHS IN LAMPLUGH

The following is now quite a famous list of records and has been quoted in various publications. They cause amusement when quoted to visitors. They can be found in the C&WAAS Transactions, Volume XLIV; New Series, 1945. The Rev S. Taylor recorded these after coming across the list of entries amongst the papers of his grandfather, who was the Rector of Lamplugh during the 1850s and 1860s. His paper was headed:

'Daily life and death - in 17th Century Lamplugh.'

"Deaths taken out of the register of Lamplugh from Janry ye i. 1658 to Janye I 1663,

Of a five bar gate, stag hunting	4
Two duels, first with the frying pan and pitchfork	1
Second between a 3 footed stool and a brown jug	1
Kild at Kelton fell races	3
Crost in love	1
Broke his neck robbing a hen roost	1
Took cold sleeping in church	2
Hanged for clipping and coyning	7
Of a sprain in his shoulder saving his dog at Culgate	1
Mrs. Lamplugh's cordial water	2
Knockd on ye head with a quart bottle	1
Frighted to death by fairies	4
Of strong October at ye Hall	4
Bewitchd	7
Broke a vein bawling for a knight of ye Shire	1
Old women drownd upon trial for witchcraft	3
Climbing a crow's nest	1
Led into a horse pond by a will of the wisp	1
Overeat himself at a house warming	1
Died of fright in an exercise of ye train bands	1
By ye Parson's bull	2
Vagrant beggars worried by Esq. Lamplugh's house dog	2
Chokd with eating (barley)	4
Old age	57

The Rev S. Taylor, who later became a canon, notes that

"The registration of Baptisms entries ceased in 1660 until 1686, except for one unusual entry in 1682. There are two marriage entries for 1661, then no more until 1686, while in the Burial section the entries ceased in 1660, and be resumed in 1684. In each case the Editor states that these missing entries cannot be supplied from the Bishop's Transcriptions during these particular years."

Rev S. Taylor states however that the document from which the records came was old but nevertheless they had a ring of truth. The records were made during turbulent times of violence. John Lamplugh returned to Lamplugh in 1658 after being heavily fined for fighting for the King's cause during the Civil War. The ordinary folk of Lamplugh, may have been

> "good wild Cumbrians, who hunted recklessly, drank deep and fought with frying pans, pitchforks, stools, brown jugs and quart pots, while their youngsters robbed hen roosts and climbed for rooks' nests. They retained their ancestors' fears of fairies, dobbies and will o' the wisps and put down many a natural death to the evil powers of harmless old women."

He questions whether it

> "might have even been the puritanical ministers and preachers who egged the parish on to the hunt and the death of witches? Was it they who added the fears of troubled consciences to the inherited superstitious fears of witches and fairies? "

And records that

> " John Myriell, who is stated in the church register to have been buried in London on August 6th 1660, may have been the ejected Anglican Rector, waiting for the King's return to regain his living, while his pulpit was occupied by stray Presbyterian or other preachers. Whether it was he or young George Lamplugh who kept a savage bull and so became responsible for the death of two of his parishioners we shall never know."(38)

HATCHES, MATCHES AND DISPATCHES!

The first and second legible baptisms dated 1581 have been given previously.

The first complete legible entry for 1581 is John Dickinson s. of Anthony of Fell Dike.

The second fully legible entry (the eleventh entry) in 1581 is Nov…Thomas Bowman s. of William Bowman of Cocklay-gill.

All entries for 1582 are complete, the first being: "June 5th Janet Tomson d. of Anthony Thomson of Kelton Head."

The heading "Married in 1581" is visible in the earliest existing register but unfortunately all the entries are illegible. There are none for 1582. The first legible marriage entry is "1583 on February 3rd (Jo)hn Bolton of Ullock in the parish of Deareham (and J)ennet Hodgshon of the psh. of Lamplugh"

The second is Mar. 23rd 1583 Rychard Lamplugh and Alice Ward.

The third is June 24th 1583 Leonard Stanwix and Annas Dickeson the wife (? widow) of John Dickeson of Streetgate.

The first burial recorded in the Registers is "1581 Oct. Mabell Hodgson o' the Green oft called Mabell Cowper the late wife of Robert Hodgson."

The second is 1581 Dec 18 John Dickinson of Streetgat.

The third is 1582 Jan 5th John Wood of Wood End, bayliff.

In 1595 there were 12 burials and in 1598 only 11 burials recorded, but when the plague visited Lamplugh in 1596/97, the burials numbered 43.

Miscellaneous entries

1582   Thomas Wood s of Richard Wood of the Woodend. (Birth)

1583   Robert Allonbie parson of Kyrkbryd and Agnes Patrickson of Stawbank. (Marriage)

1595   February 28th Mr. Tristram Warwick, parson of Lamplugh. Thus fare continueth the register during the time of Mr. Tristram Warwick, Parson of Lamplugh, so with his death ended the year 1595.

1617   August 14th Gawine Jackson: he was smuthered under hay in his bed.

1620   February 16th Thomas, son of John Lamplugh Esquire and hie shierieffe of Cumberland

1635   Robt. sonne of Jo Frear the XIII of Feb, who was birned in a lyme kilne. (the only burning that can be found)

1643   Mr. Roger Kirkbee of Kirkbee in Furnace departed this life upon Thursdaye being Novemb.2 1643 betwixt 2 and 3 of the clocke in the afternoon, and was buried at Lamplugh church upon the third daie above seven of the clocke at night. God send him a joyful resurrection. (Jane the daughter of Roger Kirkby was the wife of Colonel John Lamplugh. Roger died when on a visit to the Lamplugh home.)

1652   February 10th John Braithwaite, Rector of Lamplugh died 8th Februarie and was buried in the Chancell of Lamplugh Church the 10th day of the same month, he entered to this parsonage in August.1635, after the death of Mr. Lanclote Fletcher, late pson.

"VOLUME II 1684 (p1) BURIALS IN WOOLEN ACT"

"Burials in woolen, according to Act of Parliament, Anno regis Caroli 2di. Regis Angliae, Scotiae et Hiberniae, tricessumo. Anoque Dmi.1678. Oath made thereof and before with justice of ye Peace and with Minister of ye Word of God."

The Burial in Wool Act of 1678 was legislation intended to promote the wool trade. It stated that

" no corpse of any person (except those that shall die of the plague) shall be buried in any shirt, shift, sheet or shroud or anything whatsoever, made or mingled with flax, hemp, hair, gold or silver, or in any stuff or thing other than what is made from sheep's wool only."

Initially the priest had to certify and record in the registers that a deceased person had been buried in wool and this had to be witnessed by the churchwarden. Failure to do this resulted in a fine of £5. The Act was repealed in 1814. This did not necessarily apply to nobility or gentry in the parish, who were buried in lead coffins. These were expensive and far beyond the means of the majority of people.

The first entry in volume II 1684 records deaths in an organised and ordered sequence with the headings as below.

The parties buried within ye parish of Lamplugh in ye yeare of our Lord God, 1684	The Parties sworne	The moneth	The Justice of Peace or Minister
Mary ye wife of John Frere of High Lees	Frances Sumpton and Elizabeth Tyson	Nov 22, 1684	Jo. Lamplugh Of Lamplugh
Sarah ye daughter Jo. Jackson of Gilbert Place	Isabel Sanderson and Jane Dixon	Dec. 9, '84	Jo. Lamplugh Of Lamplugh

1686 Jan 22nd; 'Mrs. Frances Lamplugh, wife of John Lamplugh of Lamplugh Esq. departed this life upon Wednesday, being Jan. 19th 1686, betwixt eight and 9 of ye clock in ye morning and was buried in Linnen about 3 of ye clock in ye afternoon. God send her a joyful resurrection'.

1791 Dec 24th; Edward son of John Bailiff, Edge tool maker lately starved to death in the night of snow on Arlecdon Common, and of Mary his wife publickly baptized.

1792 March 24; Joshua Rawlin of Hollings, Cow doctor Eltas 88.

1804 Mary relict of William Youert of High trees; she died of a lingering disease 7th May, aged 73.

1804 John Branthwaite of Whinnow, Husbm'n and Householder, he died of a lingering disease 26th July aged 75.

1804 Mary wife of John Fawcet of Whinnow; she died of a slow disease Oct 13th, aged 71.

The medical name of the lingering or slow disease that caused twelve deaths in the year 1804 can only be guessed. It could have been due to an outbreak of diphtheria or even tuberculosis. Only medical research can reveal its true cause. The total population of the parish was then, in 1804, 535. There was another outbreak in 1892 when 26 similar burials are recorded.

1659 "Collected in the church and pishe of Lamplugh for the releife of thos distressed inhabitants of Southwark, the sume of eleaven shillings and three half pennie (Approx. 57 pence) As witness our hands Jo Myriell, minister of Lamplugh. Jo Sumpton, Wm. Harrison, Matthew Jackson, Churchwardens."

The cause of the distress is not recorded. Is it possible that Myriell had a connection with Southwark, as it would seem an unusual place for Lamplugh parishioners to choose? Myriell is recorded, as being buried in at London. However some say this may be a misprint for Lorton in Cumberland.

1661 Collected ye summe of six shillings and eleven pence for use of ye poore distressed Protestants in ye Dukedom of Lithuania. Yet another unusual place. Were protestants being persecuted there?

1688 Daniel, ye son of Lancelote Branthwaite, Gentleman, and Elizabeth d of Mr. Geo Lamplugh of Lamplugh, Clerke at Deane, ye 12th of July.

1712 ———wife of John Sewal, lost in a coal pit.

1768 The Revd. Thomas Jefferson, Rector of Lamplugh and minister of C'mouth, died Feb 3rd, buried at Cockermouth, was minister of Cockermouth in 1700, was inducted to Rectory of Lamplugh 1729 and died in 95th year of his age.

1768 May 6th; At this time was inducted Richard Dickinson, M.A. of Trinity College, Dublin, into the church, Parish of Lamplugh, by Joseph Dixon, Vicar of Brigham.

Invigilate, viri, tacito nam Tempora gressu: fugiunt nulloque sono convertitur annus.

(Translated by W H B Leech M.A. as " Be watchful, my heroes, for time flies with silent step and without sound the year changes.")

1771 Lamplugh Church flag'd, Back'd seats, pulpit in middle of the Church, Five new windows, Ceil'd overhead; placed in this old Regester because there was room to transmit it to posterity this year 1771. John Falcon, A.B. Curate.

Robert Walker, John Jenkinson. John Dixon, Churchwardens. In Falcon's hand writing. Falcon removed later in the same year to Newcastle.

On the flyleaf of the Baptism Register 1813 - 1859 is a memo that the Rev'd Joseph Gillbanks, was instituted to the Rectory of Lamplugh, by the Revd Rich'd Armistead on Thursday, the 13th of February, 1817, being promoted thereto by the kindness of the Earl of Carlisle and Lord George Cavendish. At the time Joseph Gillbanks was presented with this benefice, he was Curate at Haltwhistle, in Northumberland.

WILLS AND INVENTORIES

Wills go back to Anglo-Saxon times, but it was only the wealthiest members of society who made them. It was not until 1538 that people of more modest means started making wills. Up until 1858 the Church had the responsibility for proving wills in Probate Courts. There were three different grades of Probate Courts:

1.   The two Archbishops' Courts, i.e. the Prerogative Courts of Canterbury and Prerogative Courts of York. Canterbury was the more important of the two and dealt mostly with the southern counties whilst York dealt with Cumberland and the Northern Counties of England.

2.   The Bishops' Courts - covering a whole Diocese

3.   The Archdeacons' Court - covered just an Archdeaconry. Most wills were proved in these courts.

After 1538 wills had to be proved in one of the above courts if a person left 'goods worth mentioning', i.e. to the value of '£5 or more.' Inventories or Personal Estate listed household furniture, tools, crops, animals, cash in hand, debts owing, etc. This Personal Estate was believed to be from God and its disposal (the Testament) was therefore the responsibility of the church.

The making of a will was frequently left as late as possible, often on the actual deathbed. The dying person usually told his wishes to a clerk. He took notes and returned the next day with the written will. He read it to the testator and the witnesses and the testator would then sign it or put their marks in each other's presence. The will began with a Latin preamble naming the person and where they lived. This was then followed by

" In the name of God Amen, I .... of Lamplugh in the County of Cumberland being sick in body but of sound and perfect mind and memory, praised be God for the same. I do make this last Will and Testament in manner and form following give thanks to Almighty God for the same.

.... First I give and bequeath my soul into the hands of Almighty God my maker hoping by the glorious death of Jesus Christ to have my sins pardoned and my soul saved and my body I bequeath to the earth from where it came, to be buried in such a manner as my Executor shall think fit."

This religious wording gradually disappeared by about the 1820s. Previous to this, a clerk had been paid for the amount of writing he had done and so was pleased to make wills very wordy.

The widow was entitled to one third of the estate; another third went to the children then the debts and funeral expenses from the remaining third. Often the widow's legacy was with the proviso that she forfeited it if she remarried. The eldest son inherited the major part of the real estate, if the land was Copyhold – a form of customary tenure of land held by the lord of the manor (abolished 1922). Younger sons received real estate or a lump sum to set them up in business or apprenticeship. Daughters often got a money dowry at age 21. Sometimes they inherited land. If unmarried, they stayed with their mother or eldest brother until they married. Money was often left in trust to daughters or by using other legal devices so that their husbands couldn't get their hands on it. Married women could make a will only with their husbands' consent. It was not until the 'Married Women's Property Act of 1882' that married women were allowed to own anything. The legal position until then had been 'Husband and Wife are one person and that person is the husband.' Widows and Spinsters were always allowed to own things and therefore could make wills.

The Inventory of the deceased was normally made by neighbours of similar background and social standing who could accurately assess what the deceased's goods were worth. Until about 1750, two or three overseers were often appointed to make sure the Executor carried out the provisions of the will properly.

During the Commonwealth, 1653 – 1660, under Cromwell, the proving of wills was made a civil matter and since January 1858 all wills have been proved in Civil Courts.

The pre 1858 Wills are now usually kept in County Record Offices. Wills made in the Copeland area can be found in Whitehaven Record Office. Since 1926 there have been no geographical boundaries to the jurisdiction of probate offices. Once the will had been completed, a copy was sent to Somerset House in London. Wills are now to be found deposited at the Public Record Office, Kew. You can examine a will and buy copies at any of these places. Genealogists use wills to seek information about antecedents, which cannot always be found in church registers. The Inventories provide a fascinating insight into the lives of our ancestors, of what they owned, how they lived, and even what they wore.

INVENTORY OF AN INHABITANT OF LAMPLUGH 1707

		£	s	d
Item	His apparell and rideing gear	5	0	0
It.	Bedding and bedsteads table linen	3	0	0
It.	Arks and Chests	1	10	0
It	Pewter Brass and Iron geare	2	11	0
It	Cupboard Table Chairs fream wood	4	5	0
It	Sacks and Poaks an winowing Cloths	0	14	0
It	Meal and Malt	2	0	0
It	Husbandry gear	1	0	0
It	Cows and Horses	8	10	0
It	Sheep	2	0	0
It	Hay and Corne	6	0	0
	Total	**36**	**10**	**0**
	Debts oweing by the deceased	20	0	0
	Funeral Expences	3	0	0
	Clear	**13**	**10**	**0**

References

36. Rollinson, W.   Life and Tradition in the Lake District Dalesman publishing Co, 1981
37. Caine, Rev C.   Churches of the Whitehaven Deanery
38. Taylor, Rev S.   C&WAAS Vol. XLIV, New Series 1945

CHAPTER 11
THE CLERGY AND PARISH CLERKS

In early times the priest was paid by tithes, a system whereby every parishioner was compelled to contribute one tenth of his income, either in cash or in kind. In medieval England, village life was hard and life for the workaday priest was much the same as for his parishioners. He lived in a similar dwelling and tended his glebe land. He visited the sick and did as much as he could for the souls in his care, normally around 300 people. The priest was frequently poorly educated but he could read and write. This, on top of his religious authority, made him the person that the villagers turned to for help and guidance whatever their problems.

An old custom in Cumberland called 'Whittlegate' was accorded to the clergy (and some schoolmasters). Whittlegate meant that they were allowed to dine at the tables in the houses of their parishioners in turn, using their own whittle (knife). At the time, few households had more than one or two knives and next to none used forks, the clergy therefore brought their own "whittle." (39) This privilege became a means, used by the clergy, to eke out their scanty stipends. In some instances the 'guests' stayed a week or more at each household depending on the financial standing of the host. This custom was still being used in 1860 in some of the more remote fell dale parishes.

During the latter part of the Middle ages, guilds formed chantries where surplus priests were found employment. They were paid for saying memorial prayers for the souls of the dead. There was no chantry in Lamplugh.

For centuries it was customary for younger sons of the landed classes to become clergymen and to take over the parish on the family estate. If they inherited the estate because of the death of an older brother, some combined the role of squire and parson. They were then called a Squarson. In the 18th & 19th centuries, some clergy left their parishes in the care of underpaid curates while they often became absentee landlords e.g. Richard Dickinson.

It was in the 18th & 19th centuries that the parson's social standing rose and he became, like his medieval predecessor, the centre of village life. He sometimes set up schools and taught in them. The parsonage gardens were often used for holding fetes, bazaars and Sunday school treats. By the end of the 19th Century the parsonage set the moral, educational and spiritual standards of the village. The Victorian parsons saw that ' their' church was repaired, enlarged and furnished with new pews and heated. The reconstruction in 1870 of St Michael's might possibly have been as a result of this revival.

TWO LAMPLUGH CLERGYMEN

The following descriptions of the two clergy are taken from the book,' Cumbriana' written by William Dickinson, Kidburngill, published in 1875. (40)

"The Rev John Gregson, Senior, was curate at Lamplugh, on a small stipend, and helped it by teaching the parish school boys and girls for several years, till age and infirmity incapacitated him from active duties. He was of a mild and gentle spirit, with scarce energy enough to preserve due order among his forty or fifty restless pupils, of whom the writer was one of the juniors; the liberties were occasionally taken which he did not often resent. He was brought up a handloom weaver in Wigton, and, by a course of hard saving, had managed to fit himself for the clerical life of that day, and finally to accumulate a little property. His school day dress was of the plainest, and generally consisted of a checked linen shirt, blue duffle coat with large metal buttons, waistcoat of like cloth, drap corduroy knee breeches without braces, grey yard stockings and often clogs. These homely habiliments were supplemented by a blue linen apron, such as weavers used to wear, wound about his waist, helping to conceal the space between the waistcoat and breeches, where otherwise his linen would have been visible. This dress was seldom laid aside, except on Sundays or at funerals. At weddings or christenings, his chief change in dress was to don a black coat and waistcoat, and sometimes a white neckerchief; the surplice, having been for a taller man, doing useful service on such occasions.

Tourists had not then begun to scour the country and criticise its population; and a worthy man might wear whatever was most useful to him, and his finances could best afford without being subject to remark. The reverse of teetotalism was the fashion of that period, but he was a consistently temperate man, neither refusing to join the social circle nor indulging beyond the bounds of reason. He lived in frugal lodgings and obtained and kept the respect of his parishioners by his uprightness and meek demeanor. In person he was rather below the middlesize and broad set; and his long blue coat and rather ordinary outfit bespoke the handicraftsman, in a clean looking, ordinary working dress."

His son succeeded him in the curacy of Lamplugh.

"The Rev John Gregson, Junior, was chiefly educated by his father till fit to go to the Grammar School at St Bees. He would be a man of more than thirty years of age when ordained, and I believe his first curacy was Lamplugh. He had been pretty well grounded in the classics; and in following his father as teacher of the parish school, gave most of his attention to the advanced pupils. When I went to his school for about two years, he had a few young men of over twenty years old, educating for the Church, who made good progress under him - not greatly to the advancement of the young classes. He dressed in a rather more refined style than his father, and always wore a black coat and waistcoat, with the serviceable dark drab or olive corduroy breeches and dark grey stockings, without gaiters or leggings. He commonly wore strong calkered shoes, and was rather fond of trying their speed against those of any young men of his parish who felt disposed to give him a trial, and was not easily beaten on fair ground.

He also lived in frugal lodgings, and saved up what he could, he was a man of few words and mixed little in society, his chief amusement being an occasional game of whist, when invited to spend a winters evening with a neighbour. In summer he took long solitary walks on the holiday Saturdays. He was a good stature, and well built with little of the clerical in his appearance or demeanour, and might have been taken by a stranger for a farmer in market day dress. He had not learned to dispense with his native dialect of Wigton, and occasionally introduced his peculiarities to his reading and preaching, and more often in his sparse conversation. Now and then he had to undergo a sarcastic remark upon it, which had the effect of increasing his reticence; and being of modest retiring habits he would often have to pay the penalty for neglecting to acquire the orthodox pronunciation in his younger days."

OTHER CLERGY

1535 **Robert Layburn** was named in the Ecclesiastical survey in the 26th year of the reign of Henry VIII.

1592 **John Moorhouse** buried June 22nd 1592. He was the son of Mr. John Morehouse, preacher

1595 **Tristram Warwick** died this year

1595 – 1635 **Lancelot Fletcher** also held the living of Dean. His curate was referred to as 'Sir' Robert Pearson (Burials 1629)

1635 – 1652 **John Braithwaite**. He was buried in the chancel of the church. W Dickinson in 'Cumbriana' relates the story, which is sometimes said to refer originally to the parson.

> "John Braithwate was an inveterate rhymster. One day, meeting a servant girl, she asked if he would be pleased to let her hear one of his rhymes. He walked on a few yards, without speaking-then turned and said-
>
> "This world's come to sek a pass,
> Yan can't tell t'mistress frae t'servant lass." "

Comfort Star This clergyman has a characteristic Puritan name

1660 – 1700 **George Lamplugh.** The following statement is taken from the registers

> "1660, Dec 9th George Lamplugh, Master of Arts and Rector of the pishe of Lamplugh, according to the tenor of induction, read the 39 articles of the church of England. In witness whereof we have subscribed our names.
>
> John Lamplugh, Jos. Patrickson, Edward Lamplugh, Pickering Hewer, John Simpson, Matthew Jackson, William Harrison."

He was a younger brother of John Lamplugh, named on the tombstone in the Vestry.

1768- 1816 **Richard Dickinson** was of Trinity College, Dublin. He was a "non resident" rector. He was also Rector of Castle Carrock simultaneously and lived at

Carlisle. Isaac Fletcher wrote in his diary (41) that on April 23rd, Isaac Fletcher of Low Leys visited him.

"Got dinner and stay'd until evening. The lawsuits continue between the parish of Lamplugh & Richard Dickinson, the rector, for non residence. The declaration come. Thomas Webster is attorney for the said parish. They have Wallas' opinion upon the case which is clear against said rector. He wants to break thro' their terrier & to impose several new customs upon them respecting tithes and other pretended dues. The parish have joined and signed an article to try the cause with him."

"Richard Dickinson (1723 -1816) held the livings of Lamplugh (1768- 1816,) and Castle Carrock (1778 –1816). Further details of the dispute over his non residence have not been traced but see CWA&AS, 1960, re his attempts to impose new tithing customs." (42)

1880 **James Macarthur** became Bishop of Southampton. He was born in 1849 in Scotland and came to Lamplugh with his wife Emily who was from Carmarthen, Wales. His father was a retired paper manufacturer. At the time he was living in The Rectory, there were three servants working there. His name is recorded at the bottom of the East window as rector at the time of its installation.

1888 – 1909 **Stewart Craig**. In 1909 on September 3rd Rev S. G. Craig and Mrs. Craig were presented with a sterling silver tea and coffee set "of elegant design", an illuminated album and an inlaid walnut music cabinet on leaving Lamplugh for Lapley in Staffordshire.

"The proceedings began with a tea followed by a programme of musical items. Mr. Charles Hales, headmaster of the Parochial School, made an address and the presentation. In his reply the rector said that during the 21 years he had been in Lamplugh there had been almost a complete change of parishioners as 450 baptisms and 301 burials had occurred. Mr. John Sewell Frizington read a poem he had written especially for the occasion. This was followed by a ball 'largely attended' with a supper 'largely patronised' and a programme of "the latest and sprightliest dance music was provided by Mr. Hales, piano Miss Hales, violin and Mr. T Hayston, cornet. "Mr. Joseph Wood acted as M.C. in a courteous manner and Mr. T. Boadle made an efficient doorkeeper." All of which took place in the Murton Assembly Rooms. (43)

The later part of the boom in mining and quarrying in Lamplugh would no doubt account for the number of baptisms and burials.

1909 **Richard Haythornthwaite** was Rector for 32 years from 1909 – 1941.

The following notes were supplied by his grand children living at Seascale.

"He was respected and loved by his parishioners in and around Lamplugh whether they attended church or not. He never grumbled about the numerous miles that he had to walk and travel to cover his parish. He was mostly referred to as 'Our Rector' not 'The rector'. He had little time for rigid ecclesiastical laws and doctrines. As far as possible he escaped their rulings and 'gauged his own gait'. Where escape was impossible, if outwardly he submitted, inwardly it would be done with very ill grace! But he could preach. He would sit by the bedside of a dying parishioner and help them over that last of all human hurdles, in such a way that the 'valley of the shadow of death' lost its frightening reality, and became instead - simply "the road home." He also loved children and would waylay them coming home from school. He would talk to them but never talked down at them. They in turn responded warmly to this.

He loved his garden and on the side of the lawn there was a flowerbed in the shape of a horseshoe. That horseshoe to him was his greatest pride of the entire garden. A briar rose grew in the middle of it and round it every year were planted huge clumps of pansies and violas in blue, yellow, mauve, purple and deep brown. When he wasn't in his garden he was in the village or sitting inside the Rectory preparing his sermons and browsing through his books. He was a scholar as well as a parson.

He and his wife were financially poor with all the accompanying trials and tribulations of trying to make a thin purse stretch a long way. But neither poverty nor anything else could shake a marriage whose foundations were so rock like a quality. A small crack appeared once on a memorable occasion when his wife had been spring cleaning the drawing room. She had just hung up the fresh yellow chintz curtains over the four large windows - probably the final touch to it all - and after admiring her work completed retired for an afternoon nap, weary but elated. Unbeknown to everyone, the Rector had met the local sweep in the village and brought him home. Whilst she slept, he swept several chimneys, including the drawing room! There were no electric sweeps in those days and the method was to push the brush down the chimneys via the roof. His wife came downstairs and there was more than soot flying about! There was fury let loose and the Rector wisely wasted no time to explain but fled outside."

He represented the parish for many years as councillor on the Ennerdale Rural District Council. He was a member of the Parish Council and manager of the Parochial School. It was he who researched and listed most of the names of Rectors in the parish. He was Vice president of the Lamplugh Miniature Rifle Club. He involved younger parishioners with organisations such as The Band of Hope and the Girls Friendly Society. When he retired the parishioners and other friends presented him with a cheque and an oak cased grandmother clock with Westminster chimes. A list of the people who had subscribed to the presentation signed their names (approximately 150) and along with the gifts, this list was given to the rector. A framed picture of all the subscribers' names written in ink is still in the possession of his descendants. It is dated 30th November 1941. The clock, I am informed, is in the possession of his grand daughters at Seascale and still ticks merrily, but chimes only when it wants to.

The Miracle: - L B Ogilvie (née Haythornthwaite)

"My Father was Rector of this parish for nearly 32 years, by this time he was old and ill and long past retiring age. The World War II was in full cry and younger clergy, drawn into the network of the forces, were just about non- existent for replacements to livings.

When the second stroke hit him, his retirement seemed inevitable. He was desperately ill, he had three - quarters lost the power of speech, and he was half- paralysed. The only part of him not affected by this latest blow was his courage, which rose to meet and do battle with his crippling illness. In this struggle he was kindly helped by his neighbouring colleagues, who took services for him, and his faithful churchwardens who attended to church matters as far as they could. On all sides he was surrounded by love - a love he had very richly earned. My mother and I - above all my mother, helped to nurse him back, if not to health, at least to less weakness, so gradually he regained partial power of movement and with assistance learnt to walk again haltingly. Time inevitably slipped by and the weeks mounted. Colleagues, (some of them old too) had plenty of work on their hands with their own parishes and the difficulty of finding lay readers for the services became acute. A decision was to be made soon, and, typically he made it. He would take next Sunday's services. The doctor shook his head but bowed to a determination he had not the heart to quell. So it came about that from Monday to the Saturday night my father set about recovering a voice that had once been clear, and which was now no more than a mumble. Mother and I eavesdropped outside of his bedroom door, agonised for him. The prayers he was practising aloud were incomprehensible - even the Lords Prayer was scarcely recognisable. There was no improvement and it was Sunday tomorrow. In every sense the day when it dawned was a grey one. Rain, sleet and hail and not a break in the sky. as we helped him into hat, coat and scarf and the car that came for him.

We followed Mother to the rectory pew. I was seated directly opposite him in the choir stalls. The church lights had to be on and they showed the strain on my mother's face. I then turned and had only eyes for my father slowly coming out of the vestry on the arm of his churchwarden. He knelt to pray but this particular Sunday it seemed a longer prayer than usual. Then a strange thing happened! A shaft of sunlight from God knows where, flickered through the church and came to rest on his silvery white head. There it remained. I looked to the window that was clear glass - the rain was sheeting down! He rose a little unsteadily to his feet, the sunbeam playing around him. He looked so vulnerable. If hearts can stop beating, mine did at that moment. What was going to happen when he opened his mouth? Where was my faith? A Divine presence was in the Church that morning and its hand was upon my father's shoulder. And when he started that immortal opening from the Book of Common Prayer "Dearly beloved brethren, the Scripture moveth us in sundry places to acknowledge and confess our manifold sins and wickedness" the Master he had served all his life did not desert him in his hour of need. My father's voice rang out the length and breadth of the church - clear as a bell. Explain rationally if you can from whence came, out of a totally leaden sky, that shaft of sunlight? And why, oh why did it single out my father?

1943 was the year that **Leonard Argyle**. B.D. was inducted into the Parish of Lamplugh. He remained here for four years. The visitors' books show that he, his wife and daughter Ruth re-visited here in 1952, his address being Bearwood Rectory, Wokingham. His sons M. Argyle and Nigel Argyle have recorded visits. One was in August 1955 and the other in July 1971. The address given on both occasions was Salisbury in Rhodesia, (now Harare, Zimbabwe).

Arthur Binns was Rector from 1947 until the early 1950's. He was a good public speaker and enjoyed taking part in fund raising events for the church with his parishioners. Variety Concerts, Acting in Plays, 'Tatie Pot' Suppers, Harvest Homes, and 'Cummerlan' Neets' held in the W I Hall, are some examples. When he gave his speeches at some of these events he almost always had a humorous joke to tell about the idiosyncrasies of the clergy. His wife taught at the village school for a short while. He moved with his family to St Leonard's, Cleator and then to Crosby on Eden from whence he retired.

In 1955 **John L Howard,** a bachelor, became the Rector. He had a car but seldom used it, as he preferred to ride a bike, with his alsatian dog 'Ranger' tied on a lead attached to the handlebars when visiting his parishioners. He was a little eccentric but was loved by all the parishioners, especially the younger generation. His sermons were short and to the point and frequently referred to some pop song or music of the day. Choir practices and Bible classes were held at the Rectory in the room just right of the main entrance. They were always regularly attended and good fun. He introduced many new topics to this Bible class, which included not only the Christian religion but knowledge about other religions too. He regularly visited all the parishioners in all areas of the parish, joined in mealtimes with them, and was always welcomed. He proved to be a very dramatic singer at one particular Harvest Supper with his rendition of the song 'Cool Water' in the W I Hall. The applause was enthusiastic, loud and long and almost brought the house down.

In 1960 **Claude T. Shuttleworth** became the first vicar to be in charge of "The United Benefices of Lamplugh with Ennerdale." He had recently been married and his son was born during his five years in the Parish. He lived in the then Vicarage at Ennerdale. His task of amalgamating the two parishes together was not an easy one. He worked hard and was well thought of by his parishioners. Eventually he left the ministry and the area to return to his former work as a solicitor. He later returned to live in Egremont parish where he died.

1965 was the year when **Leslie Arthur Goddard** came to take over the parish of Lamplugh with Ennerdale. He had formerly been a curate in Egremont parish, living at Bigrigg. He organised and was involved in many memorable events in his large parish. He could always be found saying Evening Prayer every Friday about tea time at Lamplugh, and parishioners at the Lamplugh end of the parish knew they could contact him there if they so wished. Telephones were not in such popular use then as they are today. He became very involved with leading the way in which the parish was to celebrate the centenary of the rebuilding of St Michael's Church in August 1970. He organised many events, one of the most important being the 'Teaching Mission week' led by Bishop Wilson, the famous Bishop of Birmingham.

He supported and encouraged as part of the celebrations the writing of the book 'St Michael's Church, Lamplugh 1170, (1870 – 1970)'. When he moved to his next parish his health was deteriorating. When his death occurred, his wife and family brought him back to St Michael's to be buried. He was laid to rest in the new area of the churchyard which he himself had been responsible for organising whilst the Rector of the parish.

In 1974 following a short interregnum **Arthur Fountain,** took charge of the parish. When he left he was presented with a watercolour of Ennerdale Lake painted especially by Mr. R F Dickinson of Red How.

It was in 1980 that the present Vicar, **Peter J Simpson** arrived to minister in the United Parishes of Lamplugh with Ennerdale. In 1995 the parish in his charge, changed once again and became known as 'The Ecumenical Parish (Church of England) and Methodist Church of Lamplugh, Kirkland and Ennerdale.' He became the first to move into the new Vicarage/Rectory at Ennerdale Bridge. The Old Vicarage at Ennerdale was sold and is now a Bed & Breakfast establishment, which accommodates visitors, many of whom are taking part in the Coast to Coast walk.

"THOMAS LAMPLUGH, ARCHBISHOP OF YORK, 1615 – 1691"

Norman Lamplugh and Elizabeth Packenham presented in memory of their father, Kenneth Lamplugh, Bishop of Southampton from 1951 – 1971, a framed photograph of the portrait of Thomas Lamplugh at the Archbishop's Palace at Bishopthorpe, near York, to be hung in Lamplugh Church.

This Thomas Lamplugh's grandfather at one time lived at 'Skelsmore' in Lamplugh. Thomas himself was educated at St Bees School and Queen's College Oxford. He became Archdeacon of London and Dean of Rochester. He then became Bishop of Exeter during the reign of Charles II with whom it appears he had a close friendship. He was a distinguished Latin scholar. In the Rebellion of 1688 he supported James II, who appointed him Archbishop of York in that year. He was invited to take part in the coronation of William and Mary and retained his office until he died in 1691.

PARISH CLERKS

A parish clerk was a layman who assisted the parish priest in the administration of the church and also performed duties during the services such as leading the singing. He read the Gospel or the Epistle, announced psalms and led the congregation's responses, provided the starting note for the psalm on a pitch pipe and trained the choir.

> "They were often maligned persons being accused of being uneducated and opposed to change". (44)

Their office was an ancient one, traceable to Saxon times, and at one time the clerks had been men of minor holy orders. They, as a group, made a significant contribution to the music in churches in England. (44) A charter renewed by James I and later by Charles II stipulated that

> 'Every person that is chosen as Clerk of a Parish shall first give sufficient proof of his abilities to sing at least the tunes which are used in parish churches.' (44)

In 1844 an Act of Parliament deprived the parish clerks of nearly all their duties, these being given to the curates. Another Act in 1894 left them with the care of some documents and maps, but this responsibility has now been taken over by the clerks to the parish council.

Names of some of the Parish Clerks who held office in Lamplugh Parish
(Taken from the registers)

"1631 John Jackson buried Nov 1631 'the olde clerke' of Bentehowe

1697 George Mirehouse buried 2 March 1697, clarke of ye parish of Lamplugh

1736 John Stag clerk Baptism of his daughter Mary

1768 Richard Hunter, clerk 11th May Burial of his wife Elizabeth

1771 Richard Hunter parish clerk buried 19th July aged 60, wife Eliz.

1789 John Stagg Buried Aug 1789 clerk of Birkdike

1789 Thomas Mirehouse clerk 25th Oct Baptism of son Jonathan of Bankend. And his wife Mary.

1791 Thomas Mirehouse, clerk 2nd Sep Baptism of son Joseph of Gill. Wife Mary

1901 The census records of this year name John Fearon Branthwaite, Whinnah, as being the Parish Clerk"

1970 At the Lamplugh Centenary Supper and Exhibition on Oct. 2nd of that year, a public presentation on behalf of parishioners and friends was made to John Brown Stalker in recognition of his dedicated service to the church as Parish Clerk and Sexton for the previous 50 years. A portrait of him by Ronald F. Dickinson, Red How, was later hung in the church after he died on 27th April 1972, aged 76 years.

THE RELIEF OF THE POOR

Up to the early 16th century, the church, through monasteries and religious charities and with money raised from tithes, cared for the poor. A quarter of the value of the tithes was to be put aside by the priest for this purpose. After the Dissolution of the Monasteries under Henry VIII, this voluntary system disappeared and the parish became responsible for supporting its own poor. Many people became destitute because they had become deprived of their ancient rights.

In 1598 parishes were required to appoint overseers of the poor. These overseers were responsible for finding work for the unemployed and setting up poorhouses or almshouses for those incapable of supporting themselves. The overseers, who were unpaid, were elected annually at the parish vestry meeting and were given the authority to dispense the money and supervise the parish poorhouse. The overseers were also given the power to raise money by charging parishioners according to their ability to pay a tax known as the 'Poor Rate.' This was a form of income tax, but it evolved into a property tax or rate based on the value of real estate. The rate was set each Easter at the vestry meeting and was for a certain number of shillings/pence in the £. If a parish needed more money to support its poor, it increased the number of times per year that the poor rate was collected. Failure to pay resulted in a fine and sometimes prison. Every parish became a self-governing body, responsible for its own poor people. The Squire became an overseer or superintendent / parish officer for the poor relief that was given out. In Lamplugh this was a member of the Dickinson family.

Records in the registers mention many people being relieved by the parish but no reasons are given. One can only guess that the times in which they lived and social conditions, which they experienced and endured, were mostly events over which they had little control. In the late 18th century there were no large industries locally. Farming was the mainstay with some service trades such as the blacksmiths. Population numbers began to rise in the early 1800s with many examples of distress during the Napoleonic Wars among families existing on small farms. Harvests were poor, prices of food and other goods rose steeply so many people in Lamplugh had reluctantly to rely on "The Parish." A little later in 1821 the overseers accounts show 37 people out of a population of 661 received relief in Lamplugh Parish. Proportions receiving relief in similar parishes were much the same then.

The following are a sample taken from the register entries.

"1697   Henry Jackson a poor man.
1698   Ann Nutt a poor widow, who was relieved by ye parish.
1706   William Bowman, a poor man layd on the parish,
1714   Henry Myrehouse, a poor man who received alms of the parish
1732   Richard Barn a poor parishioner
1741   George Frier, formerly Clark, now maintained by the Parish
1789   John Stagg of Birkdike, parish clerk; he was supported by the parish as being very poor."

Eventually costs began to rise so that the funds available became inadequate. Many asked why so many were poor and campaigners began to work tirelessly to reform the treatment of paupers. To be labelled a pauper and to receive parish relief was considered a devastating and humiliating experience, and in any case, no one in the parish wanted to support paupers. Parishes wanted to be rid of people, if possible to another parish, or for them to be sent to work in a House of Correction. They were treated and regarded as a different class of people. To be granted any relief by the overseer it had to be proved to him that they had no shred of comfort or possessions above the line of destitution. Information by word of mouth from a reliable source, told me that even at the turn of 20th century, that one newly widowed woman, living in a cottage adjoining the Beck Smithy, was forced to sell all her furniture and most of her possessions and was then awarded a pittance on which to survive. To retain independence through a period of sickness or unemployment without the stigma of being 'on the parish' was a great achievement. Informed, responsible sources have also told me of a House of Correction, where paupers could be placed, once stood in the vicinity of Fitzbridge Wood. As yet there is no documentary proof of this.

To help retain some self-respect, at the

> "instigation of John Skelton of Rowrah, a meeting was held on the 11th June 1788, in a room at Lamplugh Cross public house, and the 23 men present decided at that meeting to form a Friendly Society. Following this meeting rules and regulations were agreed so that self-esteem in times of sickness came to Lamplugh and its neighbouring parishes" (45)

This Lamplugh Friendly Society was the second oldest in the country and was very closely connected to the church. It played a great beneficial, as well as a social part in Lamplugh's history and also in the surrounding villages. The members who proved that they were sick and unable to work received 'the benefit of the box.' A payment each week was made to them whilst ill. This club continued to exist until the introduction of the 'Welfare State' in the 1940s.

According to the Lamplugh Vestry Book in 1837 the overseers were:

> "John Dickinson, Lamplugh. Spencer Jackson, Murton. John Dixon, Kelton. Joseph Mossop, Winder."

They each received a salary of £8 per annum. The Assistant Overseer was Mr. Robinson of Dockeray Nook.

Parish records as well as family records tell us that Joseph Robinson, a yeoman farmer, living at Dockeray Nook, Lamplugh, was the current Assistant Overseer in 1875 and was presented with a silver tea service in that year. A descendant, Margaret Scanlon, still uses and treasures this tea service. It is inscribed

> "Presented to Joseph Robinson for 45 years service by the Parishioners as a mark of respect. March 1875."

His work helping and supporting the poor must have been considered worthy of their respect and appreciation. Many overseers in literature of this period are frequently portrayed as cruel, ruthless and mean men.

On April 16th 1837 the Committee for the management of the poor was:

Lamplugh	Murton	Kelton	Winder
Thos. Nicholson	John Nicholson	Thos. Bowman	Jeremiah Gunson
John Robinson	John Dickinson	John Dalziel	John Dale
John Jackson	Wm. Briggs	Henry Frears	John Yates

One record states that

> "On June 2nd a meeting at Lamplugh Cross agreed to pay Mrs. Bragg of Cockermouth 2/6d per week during illness. Relief was refused to Mr. Saul, late of Lamplugh, but recently farming at Egremont because he paid all his rates and taxes in Egremont."

References

39.	Bouch & Jones	The Lake Counties 1500 – 1830
40.	Dickinson, W.	Reminiscences of clerical life from 'Cumbriana' 1875
41.	Winchester, A. G. L.	The Diary of Isaac Fletcher of Underwood, Cumberland 1756 – 1781. 1994
42.	Winchester, A.G. L.	Footnote 195, The Diary of Isaac Fletcher of Underwood, Cumberland 1756 – 1781. 1994
43.	Dickinson, P.M.	Family papers. Newspaper clipping, Source unknown
44.	Ditchfield, P. H.	Country Folk. Methuen 1923.
45.	Dickinson, R F.	The Friendly Society of the Inhabitants of the Parish of Lamplugh & its Neighbourhood. C&WAAS – LXVI 1966

CHAPTER 12
CHARITIES, TRUSTS AND VISITORS

Like so many old charities they have become of limited value in the present day. The sums involved are very small, the objectives less relevant than when the charity was established. Administrative work can often be out of proportion to their value.

THE SCALESMOOR TRUST

This is the oldest charity, dated 1747, worth £12 a year. This sum has had to be found annually by the occupier of Scalesmoor for more than two hundred years. The remaining object of the trust is to buy Bibles and religious books for children at school in Lamplugh. One of the trustees must always be the incumbent.

THE RICHARD BRISCO CHARITY

The following is an extract from the report of the commissioners for Inquiring concerning Charities (Volume 3 pages 32 and 33) printed in 1820.

"Richard Brisco, Esq. of Lamplugh Hall, by deed dated 23rd February 1747, granted to John Brisco and Richard Lamplugh, and their heirs, a rent charge of £12, issuing out of Skelsmoor demesne lands in Lamplugh, upon trust to pay the schoolmaster of Lamplugh School for the time being, the sum of £4 yearly, for and towards the instructing of the children of the said parish, in the Christian religion: and further, upon every first Sunday in the month to pay and distribute 6 shilling, to and amongst such of the poor inhabitants of, or residing within the said parish, as they should think fit, with the consent of the owner of Lamplugh Hall for the time being; and upon further trust, to dispose of the sum of 48s, either to the said schoolmaster, or to such other person as they should appoint, for and towards the instructing in reading, writing and arithmetic, such twelve poor children of the said parish as should from time to time be nominated by the said trustees, with such consent as aforesaid; and lastly, to dispose of the rest of the said rent charge in purchasing Bibles, Common Prayer Books, and other good and religious books, to be given and distributed amongst such of the poor housekeepers in Lamplugh, or their children, as the said trustees with the like consent should think fit.

Mr. Raper, who resides at York, is now the owner of the Skelsmoor property, and Lamplugh Hall, having lately been purchased the same from Mr. Brisco.

The several sums of £4 and £2.8s.0d appear to have been regularly paid to the schoolmaster, and twelve children have been sent to him, who are appointed from time to time by the inhabitants at a vestry meeting. They are not instructed quite free, but at a lower quarterage than is paid by the other children in the school. The residue of the rent charge has been paid very irregularly. £2 was paid to the rector three years ago, to be paid out in the purchase of religious books, which was done accordingly, and they were distributed amongst poor householders: nothing however has been paid on this account for the last two years; and it is a considerable time since the sum of 6s a month has been distributed amongst the poor. In consequence however of an application having been made to Mr. Raper for that purpose, he has promised to pay the rent charge in future, and the arrears that are now due to the rector of the parish, and has requested him to attend to the proper application thereof, according to the deed of trust, with which request the rector has assured us he will comply."

A statement dated 1847 reads:

"In 1731/32 Richard Brisco Esq. Bequeathed a yearly rent charge of £12 to this Parish, to be paid out of the Skelsmere Estate & divided as follows Viz. £6 8s 0d to Schoolmaster, £2 for the purchase of books for the children & £3 12s 0d for the poor woman."

"The School endowment of this charity is now £7 4s 0d."

THE SHERWEN CHARITY

Dating from the 19th Century this charity is shared with the parish of St Michael's, Workington. The income is distributed at Christmas time to poor widows, Lamplugh's share never being more than ten pounds. In recent years there has been a slight increase. Lamplugh Parish Council nominates one trustee.

THE FLORENCE EXHIBITION

This is an educational trust, which was set up in 1924 in memory of Florence Dickinson. Investments held by the Official Custodian for Charities yield an income of about £375 per year, which may be applied in grants to any boy or girl living in the Parish of Lamplugh (and now Ennerdale) to assist them with their education at school, college or university. The Parish Council of Lamplugh nominates one trustee.

The Florence Exhibition is very relevant to present day life. Today's circumstance, when the costs of higher education are rising rapidly, young adults in the parish wishing to attend university and other similar establishments, will find it highly beneficial to receive a contribution from this trust.

THE DICKINSON MEMORIAL TRUST COTTAGES

The Memorial Houses are called Hooge Cottage and Le Plantin Cottage. These semi detached cottages are situated on the Loweswater Road near Bird Dyke, were built in 1922 and are in memory of two young men of the Dickinson family who were killed in the 1914 -18 war. The unusual names are taken from the places where the two men fell. The cottages were originally to be occupied rent-free by war widows, but they may now be let to anyone over fifty, born or resident in Lamplugh or the surrounding parishes. They are owned by the Charity

Commissioners and managed by local trustees, one being nominated by the Parish Council, the others being the Rector and Mrs. Pamela M. Dickinson. The endowment fund being very small for modern needs, the occupiers pay contributions towards maintenance and council tax.

VISITORS' BOOKS

There have been three books. Mr. & Mrs. C Sanderson, Barnsley, Yorkshire presented the first one to the church in July 1950. Mary Carr of Murton Cottage donated a second book in 1982. Now a third one is in use.

The lists of visitors who have cared to record their visit in these books contain names from many corners of the world. Some add comments and others write enquiries about different aspects in the hope that answers will be given. Comments on the peace and tranquillity, which exists within the church, are frequently made. Other visitors make requests that more information about the building be given, some are proud to note some personal facts regarding their connection with Lamplugh. Many are descendants of a Lamplugh family and state where their families had once lived. Previous parishioners even mention events they have witnessed. Some leave their e-mail addresses, asking for information, hoping that contact will be made with them.

Many people with the surname of Lamplugh and who are the descendants of the original Lamplugh family visit the parish and its church. It would appear that the Lamplugh family have descendants living in Winchester, Worcester, Warwickshire, Northumbria, Yorkshire, Cheshire Peterborough, London, Lincoln, Clitheroe, Bedford, Aldershot, Ontario and Montreal, Canada, New South Wales, Australia, and Wanganui and Kaiapoi in New Zealand to mention but a few. Kenneth Lamplugh who became Bishop of Southampton signed the book as Kenneth Southampton 23 August 1955. He visited the church on several occasions accompanied by one John Lamplugh. The signature David Ebor testifies that the Archbishop of York was a visitor too.

Many descendants of the Rogers Family live in New Zealand and they too have visited the church and noted that they came specially to see the stained glass windows donated by their ancestors.

An entry on 24 /09/ 1957 states:

"Chas. W Rose, One time P.O.W Camp Rowrah. Portinscale."

On two occasions the Rev. & Mrs E. L. Wood of St Helen's Church, Low Fell, Gateshead have visited and entered that he was 'locum tenens' at Lamplugh in 1920.

On 3/09/ 1961, S. A. Gardener of Solway Road Whitehaven has entered:

"Descendants of John Beck and Ann. First couple to be married in this church after the rebuilding." (in 1870)

CONCLUSION

A church dedicated to St Michael and All Angels has stood on the same site at Lamplugh since circa 1170. For over 830 years a building has been part of the landscape as well as being a central place for worship and part of the parish's community life. St Michael's, standing in a high and prominent position, might be likened to a sentinel on guard looking over its people below. It can be viewed from many parts of the parish. Was it by chance or was it a conscious decision of the Lamplugh family to build their hall and Church where there was already a central meeting place where others had worshipped? The answer to this we can only guess.

Today it can appear to be a windy, lonely, silent place. The setting, beneath the fells on one side and looking over the countryside and northwards across the Solway on the others, creates a certain tranquillity, which many visitors comment upon in the Visitors' Books. They frequently mention it is a " perfect setting for silent thoughts or meditation," a suitable place for a church surely!

Finally, it should be recorded that, 'The planning of Listed Building and Conservation Areas Act 1990,'have awarded St Michael's Church, Lamplugh, in Copeland, Cumbria, the status of being:

"A Building of Special Architectural and Historic Interest, and it has been upgraded to a Grade II★ listed building to reflect its special importance by the Historic Environment Case Officer in the Listing and Archaeological Branch."

BIBLIOGRAPHY

Allen.M..Hesket Newmarket

Bouch & Jones ....The Lake Counties 1500 - 1830

Bragg. M...Land of the Lakes

Bruce & Wood Family papers ....M I & K W Bruce

Caine.C..The churches of Whitehaven Deanery 1916

Collingwood. WG ....Lake District History

C & WAAS...Cumberland & Westmorland Antiquarian & Archaeology
Society Transactions

Davis. A ....Grass Roots

Dickinson. G ....Jottings by George Dickinson Red How 1828

Dickinson. J...Bound Memo Book

Dickinson. R F ....Family Papers

Dickinson. R F ....Tithing Customs of West Cumberland (C&WAAS)

Dickinson. W ....Cumbriana.

Ditchfield. PH.......................................Country Folk

Fisher. M & Smith. I................................Lamplugh Churchyard Notes and Database.

Friar. S ....The companion to the English Parish Church

Haswell. Col. F & Jackson. C......................Registers of Lamplugh 1581 – 1812 (C & WAAS)

Findler. G ....Folk Lore of the Lake Counties

Hutchinson...History of Cumberland

Jackson. W..Cumberland & Westmorland Papers & Pedigrees

Jefferson...History & Antiquities of Allerdale Ward above Derwent

Lakeland Dialect Society ....Journal 1954

Lamplugh Parish Council..........................The Parish of Lamplugh Edited by Lister. A & Marshall. B

Lamplugh Parish Council..........................Lamplugh Parish Archives

Lamplugh with Ennerdale P C ....Lamplugh with Ennerdale Parish Magazine

McIntyre. W...Lakeland and Borders Long Ago

Marshall. M.E ....St Michael's Church Lamplugh 1170 - 1970

May.T ....The Victorian Undertaker

Nicolson & Burn...................................History of the counties of Westmorland & Cumberland

Richardson. J ....The local Historian's Encyclopedia

Rollinson. W ....Life & Tradition in the Lake District

Stavridi.M...Master of Glass, Charles Eamer Kempe 1837 - 1907

Sugden. Rev E. H. ....History of Arlecdon and Frizington

Taylor. Rev. S.......................................Daily Life and Death in 17th Century Lamplugh (C&WAAS)

Winchester. AJL....................................Diary of Isaac Fletcher of Underwood 1756-1781

West Cumberland Times Newspaper

Whitehaven News Newspaper